A Spiritual Foundation for Christians

Hebrews 6:1-2

A Spiritual Foundation for Christians

Hebrews 6:1-2

Michael McKeon

© **Michael McKeon 2020**
A Spiritual Foundation for Christians Hebrews 6:1-2
1st Edition
All Rights Reserved
No part of this book may be reproduced or transmitted in any form or by any means, electronic or mechanical, including photocopying, recording, or by any information storage and retrieval system without the written permission of the author, except where permitted by law.

 A catalogue record for this book is available from the National Library of Australia

Cover Graphic: Laila Savolainen: Pickawoowoo Publishing Group
Interior and Ebook Layout: Pickawoowoo Publishing Group
ISBN 978-0-9954088-1-4 (Paperback)
ISBN 978-0-9954088-3-8 (Hardback)
ISBN 978-0-9954088-2-1 (Ebook)

Publisher: Fountain Springs Ministries
PO Box 556
Morningside, Brisbane, 4170
Queensland
Australia
www.fountainsprings.com.au

Scriptures taken from:
New King James Version © 1982 Thomas Nelson Inc.
The Amplified Bible © Zondervan and The Lockman Foundation 2015

Contents

	Introduction · vii
I	A Personal Foundation · 1
II	Repentance from Dead Works · · · · · · · · · · · · · · · · 9
III	Faith Toward God · 28
IV	The Doctrine of Baptisms · · · · · · · · · · · · · · · · · · · 52
V	Laying on of Hands · 82
VI	Resurrection of the Dead · · · · · · · · · · · · · · · · · · · 94
VII	Eternal Judgement · 111
	Conclusion · 139
	References · 141
	Other Books by the Author · · · · · · · · · · · · · · · · · 143

Introduction

Hebrews 6:

1. Therefore, leaving the discussion of the elementary principles of Christ, let us go on to perfection, not laying again the foundation of repentance from dead works and of faith toward God,
2. Of the doctrine of baptisms, of laying on of hands, of resurrection of the dead, and of eternal judgment.

Anyone without a solid Biblical foundation is prone to be spiritually confused and easily deceived by godless beliefs. The most important thing about a person is what they believe; it will influence their values, set them on a path throughout life and determine their ultimate end. There is no need to be a spiritual Tower of Pisa, waiting to fall. The study of these foundation teachings from Hebrews 6:1–2 will build a spiritual foundation in a person's life that is Biblically sound and will assist them to grow and mature in the way God intends.

This book is Biblical spirituality. Only the Word of God will feed our spirits in a way that will allow us to mature the way God has designed. Many Christians try to understand God with their mind. It is possible to engage your mind in religious theory that diminishes faith in the Word of God, and the result is spiritual dissatisfaction. You can spend many years in a church feeding from tradition and end up spiritually dissatisfied. Our spirits ache for a relationship with God, and too often they have been robbed by a theology and spirituality that is not wholly based on God's Word.

This book will help the reader give an account to others about what the Bible says about these subjects and what they believe. I always strive to minister strictly according to the Word of God and look for consistency with the Word of God in what is being taught or preached by others.

I like to see people grow spiritually and become more like Jesus. I believe that we should be able to notice a development in our relationship with God as time goes on, and that others should be able to see that development as well. In order to grow and become the people God wants us to be it is essential that we get the foundation of our belief right. It is amazing what people believe, even Christians. We need to base our belief on what God says, and then we will develop spiritually established and fulfilled lives.

I
A Personal Foundation

The gospels record where Jesus spoke about the absolute need to have a personal spiritual foundation and how to develop one. These accounts are in Matthew 7:24 to 27 and Luke 6:46 to 6:49.

Just as a building can have a strong or weak foundation, our lives can as well. Sometimes you see someone who seems to have a lot going for them. They could be intelligent, attractive, or wealthy, but they can also have a fatal flaw in themselves. It may not be easily recognizable, but it's there. There is a problem with what they believe, and, as they go through life, they just don't do as well as they could have, or through their own actions things go badly wrong and they do serious harm to themselves or others. This is because there is a problem with their spiritual foundation. According to their own thinking, everything should have gone well, but it hasn't.

The higher you are going to rise in life, the more important it is to have the right foundation. The foundation has to be right to keep the building stable through the storms we face. We need to take the time to get the foundations of our beliefs and lives right. The most important thing about a person is what they believe; this will determine the story of their life.

You can know a person at one point, but over time what they believe will determine or change who they become in the years ahead. It's especially important, therefore, for young people to choose godly friends who will encourage their relationship with God and not discourage them.

Luke 6:46–49:

> 46 But why do you call Me 'Lord, Lord,' and not do the things which I say?
> 47 Whoever comes to Me, and hears My sayings and does them, I will show you whom he is like:
> 48 He is like a man building a house, who dug deep and laid the foundation on the rock. And when the flood arose, the stream beat vehemently against that house, and could not shake it, for it was founded on the rock.
> 49 But he who heard and did nothing is like a man who built a house on the earth without a foundation, against which the stream beat vehemently; and immediately it fell. And the ruin of that house was great.

If you're serious about having a truly successful life here on earth, and then for eternity, you have to do it God's way. Jesus outlines some principles in this parable that will lead us to an established and fulfilling life.

In Luke 6:46, Jesus explains that it is not good enough to simply hear the Word of God, whether that's in church or anywhere else. He almost complains, "But why do you call Me

'Lord, Lord,' and not do the things which I say?" It's not enough to just hear, to just belong to a church or to just know that there is a God.

Remember, James said that even demons know that there is a God (James 2:19). God wants to see us respond from our heart. He wants a relationship of love with us that is proven by what we do. In John 14:24, He says, "He who does not love Me does not keep My words."

So, it's not enough to just hear the Word of God; He expects something more than that from us. He's waiting for us to do His Word. In Luke 6:47, Jesus provides three conditions that are essential to follow:

1. Whoever comes to Me;
2. and hears My sayings;
3. and does them.

First, we have to turn to Jesus. In life we have to make an effort to seek God with all our heart. It is those individuals who want to be in God's perfect will who will find it for their lives. They will develop a personal relationship with the God who is love and enter into all His promises. They are the ones who will walk on the water and out of the spiritual ruts in life.

We have to get ourselves into a position to hear the Word of God.

Proverbs 4:20-22 says:

20. My son, give attention to my words;
    Incline your ear to my sayings.
21. Do not let them depart from your eyes;
    Keep them in the midst of your heart;

22. For they are life to those who find them,
    And health to all their flesh.
23. Keep your heart with all diligence,
    For out of it spring the issues of life.

Second, we can hear the Word preached and taught in church. We can hear the Word of God through a variety of technologies. We can even hear it when we read it to ourselves. We have to make an effort to hear the Word of God. We have to do whatever it takes to overcome every obstacle to hearing from God. His Word is His will. As we listen to the Word of God we are renewing or reprogramming our thinking to think the way God thinks.

He thinks in terms of possibilities. If something's not yet created, God thinks and then He speaks it into existence. He wants us to think the way He does; nothing is impossible to God (Luke 1:37). This change of thinking, believing and living is only possible by giving attention to His Words in the Bible. The more attention we give to God's Word, the more we change our thinking to be like His. We change from thinking something is impossible to possible, from doubt and fear to faith, from sickness to healing, and from failure to victory. The more we believe and think like Him, the more we act like Him. God wants us to live achieving our potential, and the only way to do that is to act on His Word.

I used to think that God wanted me to do a whole lot for Him and He would do a little for me. I believed He would forgive my sins and I hoped to go to heaven but after that I didn't expect God to do much in my life. But as I read the Bible and had sound teaching inspired by the Holy Spirit, I found out that God will do far more for me than I was being asked to do for Him.

Third, when we desire to do the will of God with all our heart, the truth is revealed to us. It is not just a matter of studying the Bible with our minds. There are many brilliant people studying the Bible today whose spiritual eyes are only partly opened to the revelations of God because they do not seek to do His will with all their heart. They are not entering into the deeper things of God because they choose to obey God only so far. Consciously or unconsciously, they have decided that this is the limit for them. They won't walk on the water by faith with God; they like their comfort zone and won't leave it. They might be afraid of what others, even in the church, would say if they were to believe something that was consistent with the Bible but different to their religious tradition.

John 7:17:

> If anyone wills to do His will, he shall know concerning the doctrine, whether it is from God or whether I speak on My own authority.

Obedience is a key to a good relationship with God. It is the key to receiving revelation from God and it is a key to building a spiritual foundation for our lives that works.

We have to decide to obey. The choice to believe and obey saves a life for eternity. We can apply what some people call the 'rocking chair test' to our decisions. That means: will we be happy with the decisions we made in life when we look back from our rocking chair in old age?

The only sure way to build a life that will pass the test and avoid regret is the life that is built on obeying God's Word. That is the life that pleases God and is rewarded in this life and the next.

There were two people in the parable. Both went through the storm, and the pressure of the flooded stream 'beat vehemently' or violently against each life, but only one could stand up against it. Not everyone's life works out. Not everyone is happy with their life.

Some lives fail; they are a wreck. We all go through the storms of life, but the only way we can be sure that we'll still be standing when the storm is over is to have a foundation of obedience to God. We only have one go at life and we need to make it count. Choose to build a life that pleases God and you will be rock solid. Everyone born on this earth experiences storms and even crises, but there is a way of managing these storms and pressures that will ensure our success and victory – it is God's way.

Notice in verse 48 that the man "dug deep and laid the foundation". To do that you have to dig up and remove whatever comes between the believer and the 'rock' – Jesus. This man was prepared to make adjustments so that his life was now built on Jesus, who is "the Word" of God (John 1:1).

Some people believe incorrectly. For example, some people grow up in churches that teach traditions that do not come from the Bible. While others are brought up in non-Christian religions and have non-Christian beliefs and superstitions, or just believe 'junk'. All of these people need to dig up everything that doesn't come from the Bible and throw it out. That is the only way they can get down to the 'rock' – Jesus and His Word.

There is something that happens to a person when they choose to obey God. It changes them for the better in a way that the world cannot offer. So, if you want a rock-like foundation that's going to set you up for life, then get into the Word of God; get into a position where you can hear and be taught the

Bible. Get into a Bible-believing church, mediate on the Word and then do it. Live by the standard God has set in His Word. There is teaching and guidance there that applies to every area of our lives. We are told everything we need to know; how to hear from God, receive from Him and speak with Him. The Bible is the source document to absolutely everything we need to know to live above the circumstances here on earth and then live in God's loving presence for eternity.

Acts 2:42 says the early church:

> ... continued steadfastly in the apostles' doctrine and fellowship, in the breaking of bread, and in prayers.

This is the church that had good success, saw thousands come to believe in Jesus, and where people were healed, delivered and set free. This is the church that was filled to overflowing with the Holy Spirit and was a bold witness, the type of church we need to be today.

There is a spiritual foundation in the Bible that the writer of the book of Hebrews taught. Apparently, this was the foundation teaching of the early church. The writer of the epistle calls these six teachings the elementary principles of Christ.

Unfortunately, not everyone is familiar with them. The church hasn't always given this teaching the priority it had in the early church, and that God always intended it to have. There is much that God wants us to know about Himself, and I know from personal experience that studying these particular truths builds a foundation that will help you to mature spiritually.

Hosea prophesied that God's people are destroyed because of a lack of knowledge (Hosea 4:6). We have all been living below our privileges as God's children because of a lack of knowledge of His Word.

The writer of Hebrews says, in chapter 6 verses 1–2, that:

- repentance from dead works,
- faith toward God,
- the doctrine of baptisms,
- the laying on of hands,
- the resurrection of the dead, and
- eternal judgment…

…are the elementary principles of Christ. These are the foundation teachings that all believers should know, believe and obey.

II
Repentance from Dead Works

There are two Hebrew words used in the Old Testament for repent. *Nacham* (Strong's #5162), literally means to breathe deeply and implies regret. It is translated as *relent* in the New King James version and is the word applied to God when speaking about Him having a change of mind.

In the incident of the people worshiping the Golden Calf in Exodus 32, Moses pleaded with the Lord to relent.

Exodus 32:12:

> Turn from Your fierce wrath, and relent from this harm to Your people.

The other Old Testament word for repent, *shuwb* (Strong's #7725), means to turn back or return to the starting point, and is the word that most accurately describes our idea of repentance from wrong behavior.

Solomon prophesied that the Jews would be taken as prisoners to Babylon and that they would repent. He interceded to God for them, asking God to "Hear in heaven …and maintain their cause."

1 Kings 8:

47   yet when they come to themselves in the land where they were carried captive, and repent, and make supplication to You in the land of those who took them captive, saying, 'We have sinned and done wrong, we have committed wickedness';
48   and when they return to You with all their heart and with all their soul in the land of their enemies who led them away captive, and pray to You toward their land which You gave to their fathers, the city which You have chosen and the temple which I have built for Your name:
49   then hear in heaven Your dwelling place their prayer and their supplications, and maintain their cause,

Hosea also prayed for Israel to repent and return to the Lord. Hosea 14:

1   O Israel, return to the Lord your God,
For you have stumbled because of your iniquity;
2   Take words with you and return to the Lord. Say to Him, "Take away all iniquity: receive us graciously, for we will offer the sacrifices of our lips."

So, we can see that repent means to return to the Lord, to turn our hearts and our lives back toward God.

In the New Testament, the Greek word translated for repent is *metanoeo* (Strong's #3340), which means to think differently, reconsider or repent. The word repentance, *metanoia* (Strong's #3341), is the reversal of a decision, meaning repentance.

For a person to repent it means that they make a fundamental correction in their lives. It means that they are prepared to make whatever adjustments are necessary for their thoughts, words and actions to comply with the Word of God. Repentance isn't just saying you're sorry, there is a change in direction and behavior as a result of it. There is something to show for those words.

Repentance is essential to God. The call to repentance was one reason that Jesus was born and ministered on earth.

Luke 5:32:

> I have not come to call the righteous, but sinners, to repentance.

If you think you are right with God by your own goodness and efforts, you are mistaken. If you are all you need to be in a right relationship with God, He can't help you. God can only forgive the person who repents. Jesus died for sinners.

God commands repentance. We don't have a choice if we want to be in a right relationship with Him. It is an order and an obligation we have.

Acts 17:30:

> Truly, these times of ignorance God overlooked, but now commands all men everywhere to repent,

I'm sure it is pride that prevents many people from repenting. We have to admit we were wrong and that God deserves an apology. Not everyone is prepared to do that, which is foolish because everyone misses the mark; everyone does the wrong thing sometimes.

God doesn't sin, He loves and He doesn't offend; however, people do. People in a relationship need to be able to say sorry when they offend the other person, so that the relationship can bloom and grow. If either partner can't say sorry when they have made a mistake or offended in some way, the other one will suffer and the relationship will never be all it could be, if it even survives.

Part of the commission given to all disciples was to preach repentance.

Luke 24:47:

> and that repentance and remission of sins should be preached in His name to all nations, beginning at Jerusalem.

The Greek word for remission is *aphesis* (Strong's #859), meaning pardon or deliverance, forgiveness and liberty.

It is actually emotionally healthy to repent and say, "I was wrong." The person who always believes themselves to be right is unbearable. When we repent, God forgives, and the burden of guilt is lifted from a person. It is no good being dishonest with God, others and yourself by trying to deny mistakes or by saying you didn't do something wrong when you did. That sort of denial of guilt might seem to be the smart thing to do legally, but it is not ethical or emotionally healthy. God wants the truth. When children see adults lying they learn to lie as well. God always intended for people to be set free from sin and guilt, through repentance.

The New Testament Greek word for sin, *hamartano* (Strong's #264), means to miss the mark and, therefore, to not win the prize. That's a good way of looking at sin; we miss the mark of

God's best for our lives and because of that we will not receive the reward. The Old Testament Hebrew word *chata* (Strong's #2398) is similar in meaning; to miss or to forfeit. When we sin, we miss God and there are consequences.

Romans 3:23 says:

for all have sinned and fall short of the glory of God,

That is just the way human beings are; human nature is flawed, prone to sin and failure. We should be honest with ourselves and admit that, at times, we need to repent. In fact, the godly person is quick to repent rather than trying to keep justifying their actions or continue to practice sin. The smart thing to do is to run to God, not away from Him.

John the Baptist preached repentance. Matthew 3:2: "Repent, for the kingdom of heaven is at hand!" Jesus preached it, too. Matthew 4:17: "Repent, for the kingdom of heaven is at hand." And the apostles preached repentance. Mark 6:12: "So they went out and preached that people should repent."

God wants everyone to be saved and to spend eternity with Him. He does not wish anyone to be separated from Him, yet we are the ones who walk away from Him by sinning.

2 Peter 3:9:

The Lord is not slack concerning His promise, as some count slackness, but is longsuffering toward us, not willing that any should perish but that all should come to repentance.

Have you ever noticed how God seems to take His time dealing with some people? He is patient and gives us time to repent. But due season comes around and whatever people have been sowing in their lives will manifest. Suddenly, it's payday for whatever we've been doing; good or evil. Then, eventually, on a day that God has known for all eternity, we die and there is no more turning back. It is no longer possible to repent.

Repentance is unavoidable if we are to enter heaven. It will take humility on our part; we have to acknowledge that He is the creator and we are His creation. God gave us the ability to repent if and when we want to. It is a choice we all have; wise people take it.

Have you ever wondered why people repent after living a life that ignored God for many years? Even some of the best or the worst sinners will repent and turn their lives back to Jesus. It's wonderful when that happens.

Romans 2:4:

> Or do you despise the riches of His goodness, forbearance, and longsuffering, not knowing that the goodness of God leads you to repentance?

Isn't that stunning! It's the goodness of God that leads us to repentance. That tells us something about God. People think they are just on a guilt trip, but God is trying to lead them out of guilt and back to His Love. It tells us what kind of God we have.

Good preaching can lead a person to repent This is preaching under the anointing of the Holy Spirit, not shallow religious tradition. When Jonah finally obeyed God and preached to his enemies in Nineveh, people repented. I'm sure they had plenty to repent of as that society was totally corrupted by demon worship. But that's what happened; Jonah preached and the people repented.

Repentance is essential for eternal life. It is unavoidable criteria for entering heaven. Many people heard Jesus preach and didn't repent. People have a choice and, sadly, they sometimes make the wrong one.

Jesus said in Matthew 12:41:

> The men of Nineveh will rise up in the judgment with this generation and condemn it, because they repented at the preaching of Jonah; and indeed a greater that Jonah is here.

There is such a thing as godly sorrow. It is not the same as grieving without hope, which is destructive, but it is a sorrow that produces something good. If you watch the news you will see people of other beliefs, or no belief, with a sorrow without hope. You will see hysteria and depression in people's lives that doesn't come from God and it doesn't lead to anything good. It is ungodly and leads to death.

2 Corinthians 7:10:

> For godly sorrow produces repentance leading to salvation, not to be regretted; but the sorrow of the world produces death.

There can be a sorrow, a regret that will make us think about what we have been doing, and it comes from God. It is for our benefit because it will lead us to repent and get back into that right relationship with God again.

> Repentance is also a gift from God.
> Acts 5:31:
>
> Him [Jesus] God [the Father] has exalted to His right hand to be Prince and Savior, to give repentance to Israel and forgiveness of sins.

Sometimes we forget that everything we have is a gift from God, even the prompting to repent. Without God giving us that prompting, we wouldn't repent. We would just keep sinning, moving further and further away from God's love and forgiveness.

Repentance will change a person's life. Repentance will allow that person to move on with God. Once we repent it opens the way for God to lead us onto the next stage. We can't grow in a relationship with God with sin in our lives.

Jesus says in Mark 1:15:

> … Repent, and believe in the gospel.

This means make a change in your life, in what you believe and who you believe in. Repent of your sins, your unbelief, and believe in Jesus.

Acts 2:38:

> Then Peter said to them, "Repent and let every one of you be baptized in the name of Jesus Christ for the remission of sins; and you shall receive the gift of the Holy Spirit."

Peter was saying that after a person repents they start their new life and can receive the full spiritual inheritance. Be baptized, be immersed in the name and nature of Jesus the anointed savior, then go on and be filled with the Holy Spirit. This was always meant to be the normal course of growth and maturity for believers.

Repentance is just the beginning. God doesn't want us to be just saved; He wants us to grow spiritually. He wants us to grow from strength to strength and increase from faith to faith. Believers were never meant to plateau out and stop growing spiritually once we were saved. God the Father wants us to grow and become more like Jesus.

Too many people in the church don't expect to grow. They have no expectation of growth so they don't grow. The more obedient we become, the more the Holy Spirit can use us to be a blessing to others and lead them closer to the God who is Love. We're not saved just to sit and make up the numbers in a building. God wants more for us than that.

When the Apostle Paul was defending himself before King Agrippa, he gave this account of what he preached and taught to people after he met Jesus on the road to Damascus.

Acts 26:20 says:

> … that they should repent, turn to God, and do works befitting repentance.

We are saved to live a life of witness to the Lord, to help bring the harvest into His kingdom. Believers need to get involved in the lives of others to be a blessing. Do something for someone else because of Jesus. Your godly values and lifestyle of love, forgiveness, kindness, truthfulness and faithfulness will be a witness and make a difference in other people's lives.

It's not only individuals that need to repent but also whole churches and communities. There is a need for corporate repentance by churches and even of societies and nations. There can be sin committed by a church community and also at times by the wider community. This needs repentance as well. In the Book of Revelation, Jesus gave warnings to whole congregations.

He told the church in Ephesus, Revelation 2:5:

> Remember therefore from where you have fallen; repent and do the first works, or else I will come to you quickly and remove your lampstand from its place – unless you repent.

To the Church in Pergamos, Revelation 2:16:

> Repent, or else I will come to you quickly …

To the church in Laodicea, Revelation 3:19:

> As many as I love, I rebuke and chasten. Therefore be zealous and repent.

There are times when there needs to be corporate repentance led by the leadership of the church, organization or community. There is no substitute for it, God requires it.

We are told to repent from dead works. This is the first of the foundation principles. We need to do this before we can go on to the other foundation teachings listed in the book of Hebrews.

The New Testament Greek word for sin means to miss the mark or the target. When we sin, we miss the mark of what God wanted for us. We miss God's best by going our own way and rebelling.

Dead works miss the mark. Dead works can be something from any area of human life. They can be anything or have a degree of involvement God has not called us to. The crucial question is whether God called us to that activity or involvement or whether we involved ourselves without God's approval.

Some actions are not dead works of themselves; it is just that God hasn't called a person to participate in it, while other activities are already dead, especially some religious works when God has offered something better. For example, academic, social and sporting activities can be a good thing, but they shouldn't take a higher priority in our lives than the things of God.

Romans 14:23 says:

... for whatever is not from faith is sin.

We must apply our faith to every area of our lives and all our activities and involvements or it will not please God.

We've already said that sin means to miss the mark. There are churches that miss the mark by raising their own religious or political tradition and teaching above the Word of God.

The Dead Work of Religious Tradition

Jesus spoke to some Pharisees about this in Matthew 15:

3 Why do you also transgress the commandment of God because of your tradition?
4 For God commanded, saying, 'Honor your father and your mother'; and, 'He who curses father or mother, let him be put to death.'

5   But you say, 'Whoever says to his father or mother, "Whatever profit you might have received from me is a gift to God" –
6   then he need not honor his father or mother.' Thus you have made the commandment of God of no effect by your tradition.
7   Hypocrites! Well did Isaiah prophesy about you, saying:
8   'These people draw to me with their mouth, and honor Me with their lips, But their heart is far from Me.
9   And in vain they worship Me, Teaching as doctrines the commandments of men.'

There are many counterfeits in the church world. It takes a heart with a Biblical foundation to discern the difference between those that look and sound like the real thing but aren't, and those that truly are consistent with the Word of God.

Many in the church today are stuck in the rut of religious tradition. Some people give up on God because of the inadequacies of the counterfeit, thinking this is what God is really like. Others, even though they are not fulfilled in the church they attend, don't seek any deeper or further. They value or fear the opinion of other people more than they do God. They would rather stay in a church where, in their opinion, there is some status and recognition, rather than step out on the water to where Jesus calls. That's where Jesus is calling; where there may be no earthly support or where others may think you've gone too far.

They limit God's ability to work through them by the traditions they religiously but unscripturally cling on to. If a belief or a practice isn't based on the Bible it doesn't come from God.

Generally speaking, churches are a mixture of scripture and human tradition. Often, these traditions have been included with good intentions, but they can take on an authority of a Biblical doctrine that does not belong to them.

The traditional denominations are losing their status and members because in this day and age people want more than tradition, people want something genuinely spiritual. We are a spiritual being, made in the image and likeness of God, and we crave to be fed and filled spiritually. We want to connect with God and the only way to do that is God's way of doing things in His Word.

When I was a young man, I studied to be a Catholic priest. I trained for four years but didn't get ordained. I was conscientious but spiritually unsatisfied. In the end God was able to get through to me that this was not His best for me.

We need the God-ordained ministry He set in the church. This is the only type of ministry that will lead the body of Christ to maturity and bring spiritual fulfillment.

Ephesians 4:

11 And He himself gave some to be apostles, some prophets, some evangelists, and some pastors and teachers,
12 for the equipping of the saints for the work of ministry, for the edifying of the body of Christ,
13 till we all come to the unity of the faith and of the knowledge of the Son of God, to a perfect man, to the measure of the stature of the fullness of Christ;
14 that we should no longer be children, tossed to and fro and carried about with every wind of doctrine, by the trickery of men, in the cunning craftiness of deceitful plotting,

15 but, speaking the truth in love, may grow up in all things into Him who is the head – Christ –
16 from whom the whole body, joined and knit together by what every joint supplies, according to the effective working by which every part does its share, causes growth of the body for the edifying of itself in love.

This is the New Testament model of ministry that God designed for the church, and we should build our churches based on that. The operation of these ministry offices promotes growth of the individual believers and of the church as a whole.

In the Bible, priests offer sacrifice for sin. In the New Testament church there are no priests because there is no more sacrifice for sin that can be offered.

In Matthew 18:16, Jesus quotes Deuteronomy 19:15 when he says, "by the mouth of two or three witnesses every word may be established." Here are three witnesses from Hebrews, there are others as well, showing that there is no more sacrifice to be offered for sin. Jesus has done it 'once for all'.

Hebrews 9:12:

Not with the blood of goats and calves, but with His own blood He entered the Most Holy Place once for all, having obtained eternal redemption.

Hebrews 9:28:

… so Christ was offered once to bear the sins of many.

A Spiritual Foundation for Christians

Hebrews 10:10:

By that will we have been sanctified through the offering of the body of Christ once for all.

The spirit of anti-Christ resists the Spirit and ministry of Christ. Remember that Christ is Greek for 'the anointed and his anointing'. The spirit of anti-Christ will resist anyone or anything connected to the anointing of God.

Many believers still don't believe it is possible to be filled with the Holy Spirit with the evidence of speaking in tongues (Acts 2:4). They don't know they can have the gifts of the Spirit operate through them the way the early church experienced, as written in 1 Corinthians 12.

Remember, God spoke through Hosea 4:6: "My people are destroyed for lack of knowledge." Many people are living below their rights as children of God not receiving their full inheritance and sometimes dying before their time. This ignorance of God suits the devil.

Every time revelation has been given to the church on an aspect of the anointing or empowering of God for His people, it has been fiercely resisted by some members of the church because of the influence of the anti-Christ. Some ministers resisted the teaching and work of the Holy Spirit, and some Christian bookshops have refused to stock literature on the anointing of the Holy Spirit.

We know what a dead service feels like. Death has already struck at a funeral but even the service can be spiritually dead if there is no anointing on the minister and the service they conduct. If there has been insufficient openness and obedience to God, He will stay away. He will not manifest His presence, His peace or His glory if there is little obedience to His Word or worship from the hearts of people.

The Dead Work of Inappropriate Activity

People can become involved in dead works through involvement in worldly activities. They are not necessarily immoral, but if God hasn't called us to be involved, it's dead works. As explained earlier, God wants us to grow spiritually but we can't if we are involved in activities that He has not directed us to devote our time to and be involved in.

An example is inappropriate political action. A number of years ago I joined a political party. I believed that this party had the best values and policies for most Australians and, therefore, I should be involved. As time went by I became dissatisfied.

After I was filled with the Holy Spirit, I gradually found it more and more difficult to belong to the political party. That wasn't my calling and I just didn't belong there. It wasn't just that particular party either; I didn't belong in any political party at that time. It was dead works to me. I can't say that I will never belong to a political organization again, that's up to the Lord. I would like to be obedient and join if I felt the Lord was leading me to do so.

Actually, I believe more Christians should seek the Lord about being involved with politics, first so that they become better informed, and, second, so that they can make a godly contribution. We need Christian politicians who will speak out and take a stand on God's Word and values no matter what party they belong to, and not just blindly follow the party line. We need government policies that have been birthed and influenced by the wisdom of God. The management of the country is too important to leave to people who are hypocrites or who do not know God.

The Dead Work of the Tradition of Men

The Apostle Paul had been a Pharisee steeped in religious tradition until the Lord knocked him off his high horse and opened his eyes.

He warned in Colossians 2:8:

> Beware lest anyone cheat you through philosophy and empty deceit, according to the tradition of men, according to the basic principles of the world, and not according to Christ.

The "tradition of men" does not lead to God's best. Human tradition in whatever form is not spiritually fulfilling. You cannot substitute it for the Word of God because it will rob a person of a fulfilling relationship with God and their inheritance here in this life and the next.

The "tradition of men" is not restricted to one denomination but would try to infiltrate all denominations. It will dilute the Word of God and the leading of the Holy Spirit, confusing a believer. Traditions may be introduced with good intentions, but they can be used by controlling influences that try to gain and maintain their own power within a church and exclude the authority of the Word of God and the Holy Spirit.

Tradition doesn't lead people to Jesus. You'll notice that the more a person is trained in a tradition, the harder it is for them to talk about Jesus and the Word of God.

Tradition is the substitute the devil subtly holds out to the church and the world to dilute the anointing, which destroys yokes and breaks bondages that have people bound. It is only the anointing that will break satanic strongholds over a person's life, and the anti-Christ will rob the church of that anointing power.

When Paul wrote 2 Timothy 3: he said;

1. But know this, that in the last days perilous times will come:
2. For men will be lovers of themselves, lovers of money, boasters, proud, blasphemers, disobedient to parents, unthankful, unholy,
3. unloving, unforgiving, slanderers, without self-control, brutal, despisers of good,
4. traitors, headstrong, haughty, lovers of pleasure rather than lovers of God,
5. having a form of godliness but denying its power. And from such people turn away!
6. For of this sort are those who creep into households and make captives of gullible women loaded down with sins, led away by various lusts,
7. always learning and never able to come to the knowledge of the truth.

Culture is also a tradition of men that can become a dead work when it conflicts with God's Word.

In John's Gospel, chapter 4, there is a wonderful example of Jesus transcending culture, race and gender relations. He was talking to a Samaritan woman at a well. The Jews held Samaritans in contempt. It was not normal or culturally appropriate for a Rabbi to be speaking to a woman, especially a Samaritan woman. His disciples "…marveled that He talked with a woman." (John 4:27). But Jesus had work to do. He was about His Father's business, leading people into the kingdom of heaven. He refused to let a tradition of man, a tradition of culture, prevent Him from ministering salvation.

Cultures are not perfect or infallible. Some people place culture above God and worship and obey it before God and His Word. Culture can be questioned, modified and set aside. God will set us free from any aspect of a culture that works against His will and is a hindrance in our walk with Him.

We all have an identity imprinted on us from our culture, and we are not meant to lose that, but God wants to separate His children from anything in a culture that is a barrier and a hindrance to walking in a deeper relationship with Him and receiving everything He has for us.

Praise God, He wants to forgive us and set us free from anything that would separate us from Himself. The book of Hebrews tells us to repent from dead works. We need to be honest with ourselves and repent, and God will forgive us. He promises that.

1 John 1:9

> If we confess our sins, He is faithful and just to forgive us our sins and to cleanse us from all unrighteousness.

So no matter what mistakes we've made and how much we've missed the mark with God, we can always turn back and He will always forgive us.

III
Faith Toward God

What is Faith

Men and women are made in the image and likeness of God (Genesis 1:26). We are made like God, in the God class of being. We are different from angels and any other created being. We can operate by faith. We may have similarities with other forms of life on earth. For example, animals have emotions and can communicate with each other, monkeys can walk around on two legs and pick things up with their hands, but we are the only type of creature that has a spirit and the capacity to communicate with God and operate by faith. That's something that sets us apart.

The New Testament Greek word for faith is pistis (Strong's #4102), and it means moral conviction of the truthfulness of God, assurance, belief, faith and fidelity.

We often hear the word faith, unbelievers will even use it, but what does God mean by faith? The Bible gives a definition. Hebrews 11:1:

> Now faith is the substance of things hoped for, the evidence of things not seen.

The Amplified Bible translation of Hebrews 11:1 says it this way:

> Now faith is the assurance (title-deed, confirmation) of things hoped for (divinely guaranteed), and the evidence of things not seen {the conviction of their reality-faith comprehends as fact what cannot be experienced by the physical senses}

If you have faith in God to perform His Word, you have already grasped what you are believing in Him for. You have hold of it in the spiritual realm, and God considers your faith to be concrete evidence of something that is going to manifest in the physical realm.

Faith bridges the gap and opens the way between two worlds; the natural and the supernatural. To have faith in God is to reach out into the supernatural, to transcend the natural order and live above the circumstances or symptoms you are experiencing.

Where Does Faith Come From

Romans 12:3:

> ... as God has dealt to each one a measure of faith.

Faith is a spiritual attribute and can only be received from God. When Paul wrote to the church in Rome, he said that the measure of faith is given at the time a person decides to believe Jesus is God and accept Him as their savior. Faith is not something we are born with, it is something we are born spiritually with. Even the ability to believe in God and His Word is something that we receive from God when we choose to believe and worship Him.

This scripture means that an equal measure or amount is given to each person when they become believers and are born into the family of God.

In John 3:3, Jesus said:

Most assuredly, I say to you, unless one is born again, he cannot see the kingdom of God.

The words "born again" have also been translated "born from above". This is the point in a person's life when they are given the gift to believe in God. The person chooses to believe and then God gives the ability or the grace to believe Him and His Word. Faith is initially given in equal amounts to every person who chooses Jesus as their God. The initial gift cannot be generated without God's grace, His undeserved gift.

How Does Faith Grow?

The Bible says that faith comes or grows by hearing God's Word. This is the Bible way for us to increase our faith. The more we hear the Word of God then the more faith we will have. Our faith will grow if we are in a church that preaches and teaches from the Bible. The most important step to growing spiritually is to be part of a Bible-believing church. As I have said, there are churches and ministers who will elevate a tradition or perhaps a person above the authority of God's Word, and that doesn't please God or increase anyone's faith.

Many of us grew up in churches and still didn't have much faith. I know some people had more faith than I did but I didn't know what I could do about it. There was no one who could

teach me about faith and how to develop more of it. But when we look to the Bible, God's own Word tells us what we need to do.
Romans 10:17

> So then faith comes by hearing, and hearing by the word of God.

The only way that faith increases is by "hearing, and hearing" the Word of God. The Bible doesn't say to pray for faith, it says to listen and listen to God's Word. We can read to ourselves, even to someone else, and hear the Word. We can hear the Word of God preached and taught in a variety of media formats. Take every opportunity to hear God's Word and your faith will grow all the time. That way, we can be like Smith Wigglesworth, the great Pentecostal minister from the first half of the 20th century, who coined the expression and lived in "ever-increasing faith". I'm sure it would please God if we would increase our faith in Him by listening to Him more.

Why is Faith Important to God?

Faith is important to God. Just as a father or a trusted friend wants to be believed, God wants us to believe Him. He wants us to live by faith in what He says.
It is faith that gives a person the right relationship with God. John 3:16:

> For God so loved the world that He gave His only begotten Son, that whoever believes in Him should not perish but have everlasting life.

Michael McKeon

Acts 16:31:

So they said, "Believe on the Lord Jesus Christ, and you will be saved, you and your household."

Romans 3:

21 But now the righteousness of God apart from the law is revealed, being witnessed by the Law and the Prophets,
22 even the righteousness of God, through faith in Jesus Christ, to all and on all who believe. For there is no difference;
23 for all have sinned and fall short of the glory of God,
24 being justified freely by His grace through the redemption that is in Christ Jesus,
25 whom God set forth as a propitiation by His blood, through faith, to demonstrate His righteousness,

Romans 4:3:

For what does the Scripture say? "Abraham believed God and it was accounted to him for righteousness."

Ephesians 2:

8 For by grace you have been saved through faith, and that not of yourselves; it is the gift of God,
9 not of works, lest anyone should boast.

God wants His people to live by faith. We are meant to involve God in everything we do by believing in Him and His Word to us to protect and provide for us. God wants to be involved in our lives, all the time.

The prophet Habakkuk said 2:4

> ... But the just shall live by his faith.

And the writer of Hebrews repeated it in chapter 10:38. In fact, anything we do, trusting only in ourselves without trusting God to help us, is offensive to Him.

Hebrews 11:6:

> But without faith it is impossible to please Him, for he who comes to God must believe that He is, and that He is a rewarder of those who diligently seek Him.

We really haven't properly understood how much God wants to see us living moment by moment, day by day, trusting Him. As we grow in that revelation we will grow in our revulsion of any kind of manipulation that tries to 'fix' what we desire or need without God being involved.

The apostles wanted Jesus to increase their faith for them. They knew that faith unlocked the power of heaven and they wanted more. Jesus answered them as follows.

Luke 17:6:

> If you have faith as a mustard seed, you can say to this mulberry tree, 'Be pulled up by the roots and be planted in the sea,' and it would obey you.

Michael McKeon

A little faith will do a lot. We need to use the faith we already have, which may not seem like much to us at the moment, but our little faith will make a difference. As we use the faith we already have, and position ourselves to keep hearing God's Word, its effectiveness will grow. You will build faith muscles by starting with the faith you have and feeding it.

Manipulation is out for the Christian. There is no need to bend the rules or break the law to succeed or prosper. God can only bless us while we abide by the law and play fairly in whatever we do. Taxes are a good example. God expects believers to pay our rightful taxes. Jesus paid His (Matthew 17:24–27), and it is wrong for Christians to avoid paying taxes by breaking the law. God is well able to prosper us when we are paying our fair share.

We haven't understood just how close a relationship God desires to have with His people. He wants to be included in everything we do. We need to be aiming to live a life that depends on God's ability and not our own, and He will bless and prosper us.

Romans 14:23

… for whatever is not from faith is sin.

The first time I heard that scripture it set off a shockwave inside of me. How could that be, I asked myself, because I was still trying to justify myself by being 'good'? I really wasn't using much faith in my everyday life and that showed me how much I'd missed God's way of doing things. It was an uncomfortable realization. I imagine the Apostle Paul felt a greater shock and did his best to teach the revelation to the church in Rome and everywhere else he ministered.

God didn't create us to be independent of Him. He wants to bring in the harvest on the earth with us and through us. Remember, the believers now make up the 'body of Christ'.

As we can see from these scriptures, faith is extremely important to God. It always has been – right throughout the Bible – and for believers to have the mistaken idea that they will be saved by their good works is a serious misunderstanding. Their vain attempt to perfectly keep the commandments is contrary to the emphasis and teaching of God's Word. Why would faith be so important in every area of a person's life if redemption can be achieved by keeping the commandments alone? This reveals a misguided understanding of what God has been saying throughout His Word. There is a spiritual blindness at work here.

We Can Only Understand God by Faith

Hebrews 11:3:

> By faith we understand that the worlds were framed by the word of God, so that the things which are seen were not made of things which are visible.

In fact, the only way we can understand or accept creation and the Bible is by faith. Don't try to reason it. Creation is a creative miracle; it is unreasonable, it is miraculous. In the Bible there are many things we can't understand with our minds. How could Methuselah live to 969 years? How could all the animals have fitted into the Ark with Noah and his family? Don't worry about it; God created the natural laws of the universe and he can cause miracles or exceptions to the natural order anytime He chooses. As I began to witness the gifts of the Holy Spirit in operation – prophecies that came true, tongues and interpretations, discerning of spirits, gifts of healings – I had less trouble believing anything God said in His Word.

Science is not infallible and it is not the final authority. It is a limited body of knowledge that is liable to change and vary as new discoveries are made and verified. The theoretical and practical boundaries of knowledge keep extending with new discoveries. Old theories are challenged and new ones are put forward. There have been huge advances in electronics, computer and medical science in recent years that would never have been thought possible a short time ago. Science and all disciplines of knowledge are still learning.

There are many Christians around the world trying to understand God and His Word intellectually. God is a Spirit and you need to approach any study of God and what He says with your spirit. When theology attempts to understand God with the human intellect, under the heavy influence of religious tradition rather than the Word and the revelation of the Holy Spirit, it complicates the search and usually diminishes the faith of the person in the process.

I don't worry about something I don't understand in the Bible. I have come to realize that there are some things that God has not revealed to me yet, but if I keep seeking Him and the truth of His Word, I will come to understand more. The Bible doesn't tell us everything but it does tell us everything we need to know. I believe that those things we don't understand in this life will be revealed to us once we come into the presence of God in His kingdom.

A Spiritual Foundation for Christians

God is Love but He is Moved by Faith

God is love but He responds to faith. God is not moved by need. God's people are under attack all the time and can have all kinds of needs; emotional, physical, spiritual and financial. However, unless we put our faith to work in a promise from His Word and act on it, we will never receive from God and have our needs met.

There have been many Christians who were needed by their families and communities but whose health failed and who died before their time. We don't know everything. That is a matter between them and God.

God is love but He is moved by faith. Not all Christians are brought up being taught about faith. If you were brought up in a 'traditional' denomination, your knowledge and level of faith would be limited. However, the Bible tells us that faith is very important because without it we cannot please God. All of our good works won't amount to much in God's eyes if they don't involve faith in Him.

There are a lot of people in the church doing a lot of things by their own power, and by depending on the resources of this world to achieve something that God would like to be more involved in. He would like to see us depend on Him for everything we do and for everything we need.

Often, members of the church think that people were healed in Jesus' time because it was Jesus who did the praying, so they were instantly healed. But when you look at the scriptures you can see that this wasn't the case. The faith of the people involved played a vital role. There are many instances in the ministry of Jesus where if people didn't have faith to be healed then they wouldn't have received their healing. When Jesus healed two blind men, He said the following:

Matthew 9:29

Then He touched their eyes, saying, "According to your faith let it be to you."

The woman with the hemorrhage for twelve years demonstrated her faith:
Luke 8:48

Daughter, be of good cheer; your faith has made you well. Go in peace.

A man with a disability in his feet received his healing because of his faith:
Acts 14:

9   This man heard Paul speaking. Paul, observing him intently and seeing that he had faith to be healed,
10 said with a loud voice, "Stand up straight on your feet!" And he leaped and walked.

Faith is the only pathway to receive from God; there is no other way. You can't buy it and you can't earn it; you can only believe for it. When we pray, we must believe that we receive at the time we prayed and asked God.
This is what Jesus taught in Mark 11:24

Therefore I say to you, whatever things you ask when you pray, believe that you receive them, and you will have them.

Believe at the time you pray that you have received the answer in the spirit realm, and then thank God for it until it manifests. When you have laid hold of what you have requested by your faith, don't let go.

In Matthew 11:12, Jesus said:

> And from the days of John the Baptist until now the kingdom of heaven suffers violence, and the violent take it by force.

Jesus is saying that we need to have a violent determination about our faith. We need to be so strong in our belief that it has a great force. There was never a time when believers could afford to be weak in their faith. A weak faith could cost someone their healing, their marriage, their children or their life. Be determined, be violently strong in your faith and receive everything you pray for.

Make a decision to develop a level of faith that is so confident that it is aggressive; it's warlike and no devil in hell can stop you receiving what belongs to you in God's Word.

Faith, Faithfulness and Worship

Faith, faithfulness and worship are related.
Hebrews 10:

> 22 let us draw near with a true heart in full assurance of faith, having our hearts sprinkled from an evil conscience and our bodies washed with pure water.
> 23 Let us hold fast the confession of our hope without wavering, for He who promised is faithful.

What is the link between faith in God and faithfulness? Having faith in God is being faithful to Him. Believing His Word, believing He is able to perform His promises is being faithful to Him as God. When you have faith in God you believe that He is able to perform miracles, to do what is humanly impossible, you believe that God is more knowledgeable and powerful than any other power in the universe.

We worship an unseen God because we believe He is supreme over all else, and we are faithful in this relationship that He is our God and we are His people. If we don't have faith we don't believe that He is able to perform His Word.

Hebrews 11:6:

> But without faith it is impossible to please Him, for he who comes to God must believe that He is, ...

Therefore, faith and worship are closely linked. It is impossible to please God without faith, it is impossible to worship a God we do not believe in. The more we believe in the God of Love, and the more we want to live for Him and offer our praise to Him, the higher our worship will rise. We do this without seeing His form, without hearing His voice or the heavenly choir, singing Holy, Holy, Holy. We worship God by faith.

Faith and Rest

Hebrews 3:

> 12 Beware, brethren, lest there be in any of you an evil heart of unbelief in departing from the living God;

15   …"Today, if you will hear His voice, do not harden your hearts as in the rebellion."
18   And to whom did He swear that they would not enter His rest, but to those who did not obey?
19   So we see that they could not enter in because of unbelief.

An unbelieving heart is an evil heart in the sight of God. He is not pleased with that person and there are consequences for the disobedience of unbelief. We all need to walk in the light that we have. We need to live a life of obedience to God, and that starts by believing Him. The prophet Samuel said that obedience was better than sacrifice (1 Samuel 15:22).

There is rest and reward with God; however, it can only be entered into by faith and obedience. Without faith in God and His Word, there will be no rest and no reward. The only way to live in satisfaction and rest for all eternity is to live with God in your life.

Many people hear the Word of God regularly. Many ministers preach something of the Word, even daily, but it doesn't profit them. Why? Because it is not being mixed with faith. It is absolutely incredible to think of all those 'church goers', which is what many of them are because they are not believers, going to church 'religiously' but not believing in God's Word.

They haven't been encouraged or taught to believe; therefore, they can't. That form of church really has more in common with a social club than a Bible-believing church. Paul advises that we stay away from people and churches that don't have faith in God and His ability to work miracles in our lives. That seems a bit strong but that is how he felt about them.

2 Timothy 3:5:

... having a form of godliness but denying its power. And from such people turn away.

So, we see in the Word that some could not enter into God's rest because of unbelief. In the heart of every person is the need to have a place to call home. It is the place where they feel safe and secure and are able to rest from the pressures of life. Home is that place where you belong. The rest that God offers is the eternal home our spirits desire; however, it is only entered into by faith in God and His Word.

Hebrews 4:

1. Therefore, since a promise remains of entering His rest, let us fear lest any of you seem to have come short of it.
2. For indeed the gospel was preached to us as well as to them; but the word which they heard did not profit them, not being mixed with faith in those who heard it.
3. For we who have believed do enter that rest, as He has said; "So I swore in My wrath, 'They shall not enter My rest,'"

The Word of God must be 'mixed' or combined with faith by the hearer for it to work for them. To enter the rest of God from all the work and challenges of this life you have to take the risk and believe that what God said is true. Everything and everyone around you may be telling you that it is impossible for God's promise to be true, but you have to decide to take the risk and trust God. Without taking the 'risk', believing in God and then in His promises, you are guaranteed not to make it to heaven and the rest that is promised in the presence of God.

When Peter walked on the water, he was engaged in 'faith-taking behavior'. Without enough faith it was a risk. He could have sunk like a stone to the bottom of the lake, but for a moment he believed God and was walking on the water. Faith steps out and speaks in faith in spite of the circumstances.

Faith Turns on the Tap

Romans 5:

1. Therefore, having been justified by faith, we have peace with God through our Lord Jesus Christ,
2. through whom also we have access by faith into this grace in which we stand, and rejoice in hope of the glory of God.

Grace is the undeserved gift of God. The only way to enter in and receive any of God's gifts is by faith. The more faith, the more God is pleased and the more you receive. On one occasion, when Jesus heard a centurion say:

Matthew 8:

8. ... But only speak a word and my servant will be healed.

Jesus was amazed, and said He hadn't:

10   … found such great faith, not even in Israel!

The most faith Jesus had seen up to that time came from someone who wasn't a Jew. He was surprised at the level of faith of the centurion and He healed His servant without visiting the house. The centurion decided to believe Jesus could heal his daughter with all his heart. That's the way we've got to be.

Being moderate, lukewarm, and balancing faith with unbelief disguised as reasonableness, doesn't impress God. Faith impresses God and gets His attention. The more faith you put to work, the more of His attention you have.

Faith allows and enables a person to operate in the supernatural. The believer has access to God's supernatural by believing His Word and acting upon it.

Any person who chooses to believe in the God of the Bible and His promises is able to act in the realm of God's supernatural as His child. This is what God always intended for His children, that they would 'live by faith' and not by their own efforts.

Faith will set you apart from the people around you that don't live by it. They are living and thinking to a different set of rules with a different set of boundaries. People with little or no faith are limited to the circumstances and resources of this natural world. Whereas people of faith have learned to depend on God's ability, not their own, and that's why they can throw mountains of trouble into the sea, walk on water of impossibility and quench fiery attacks from the trouble maker.

It's not because they have some natural advantage, it's only because they've learned to believe God. Believing the Word of God and acting on it makes spiritual power available.

Jesus told Jairus, the father of a dead girl, in Mark 5:36:

Do not be afraid; only believe.

Jairus, the ruler of a village synagogue, may have never witnessed anyone being healed before. However, when he was told his daughter was dead, Jesus told him to just believe. Jairus decided to go up a gear and believe God for something he'd only ever read in the Word of God, and something he'd never seen. He believed and he received. His daughter was raised from the dead.

That's the way God wants us to believe as well. He wants us to have a lifestyle of faith that grows and grows so that we can turn the tap wide open and receive everything we need by using our faith.

Faith Working by Love

Faith on its own isn't enough. God wants to see it mixed with love. You can try to develop faith that will move mountains, but if you don't develop love for others, your faith won't impress God. Everyone has needs but He will only work when people believe and act in love. Faith works by love.

Galatians 5:6 says:

For in Christ Jesus neither circumcision nor uncircumcision avails anything, but faith working through love.

Paul was stating that faith works by and through love. Being circumcised and trying to be justified by keeping the Ten

Commandments won't make faith work for you. Being circumcised or uncircumcised doesn't make any difference; only applying love to your faith will make a difference. God wants to see love in the heart of a believer, and that's what makes faith effective.

It is no use trying to develop a faith that will move mountains without a heart of love. God is not interested in that kind of faith. There are people wondering why their faith isn't working. One reason could be that they don't walk in love.

1 Corinthians 13:2:

> ... and though I have all faith, so that I could remove mountains, but have not love, I am nothing.

It is possible to try to develop faith for the wrong reasons. It is a good thing to desire mountain-moving faith but not want it for your own exclusive benefit. Desire an increase in the things of God to be a blessing to others, not just to be blessed. When God sees that you want to share what you receive, He will bless you.

Love always does something for someone else. Love is aware of the need of others and looks for ways to meet that need. True love that comes from the heart of God will motivate a person to take action that will help others, especially when they are in need.

Sometimes I've heard people say that faith is a private thing. They were sold a lie from the devil. Our faith in Jesus is meant to be shared. Just as Jesus was involved in the lives of others showing the love of God, we should be also.

Faith Without Works is Dead

God expects us to be doing something about what we believe. James 2:

14 What does it profit, my brethren, if someone says he has faith but does not have works? Can faith save him?
15 If a brother or sister is naked and destitute of daily food,
16 and one of you says to them, "Depart in peace, be warmed and filled," but you do not give them the things which are needed for the body, what does it profit?
17 Thus also faith by itself, if it does not have works, is dead.

God wants to see some action, not only on your own behalf but also for the 'profit' or benefit of others. Believe big to be a witness and a blessing for the needs of others. God wants to see us involved in the faith projects of others in the church in practical ways. Give time, money and practical support.

Some believers and churches have been good at being 'spiritual' but haven't taken as much interest in the practical material needs of people. Some Christians and ministers only want to know about the people who are making it in life and don't want to come down to the poor and needy. Other believers and churches emphasize caring for the physical and material needs of people and are under-equipped to meet their spiritual needs.

Jesus expects us to get involved and help people who need help. They can be unloving and ungrateful of our effort but it doesn't go unnoticed by God. There are many reasons why people are lacking; sometimes it is and sometimes it is not their fault. Sometimes there needs to be something done at a government level to create better policies to provide a social safety net to develop a more civil and Christian society. This would be a witness to non-Christian societies that don't provide effective care for their vulnerable people. The core values of the churches and organizations we belong to need to be consistent with the teaching and values of the Bible.

This scripture in James says that our faith has to be put into action to receive from God. Believers should be givers and doers. Many times, people won't receive their healing if they don't try to do something that they couldn't do before. For example, if they had a problem with a part of their body, they should start doing something they couldn't do before. When God sees you putting your faith to work, He will honor that.

When we are believing for something and waiting for it to manifest, we should start making preparations for it. When a woman is having a baby, she starts getting the things the baby will need before it arrives. The family starts buying baby clothes and toys. They get the room ready. They start thinking of a name and thinking about the future for that child. Well, that's the way believers should be while they're pregnant with faith; getting ready for the manifestation of their faith. Make the preparations for the manifestation of your blessing and the changes it will bring into your life.

It's no good praying to and believing God for something yet not preparing for it. A positive confession of your healing is acting on your faith. You can speak out the answer to your prayer as a testimony and that is acting on your faith. You can say it to yourself or you can proclaim it to the world, "Thank you, Lord", for what you asked for, and God is listening and He counts that as acting on your faith.

James 2:26:

For as the body without the spirit is dead, so faith without works is dead also.

Faith that doesn't get involved to make a difference in other people's lives is dead. It's a joke. You can say what you like; God is not interested in that kind of religion.

Faith Speaks

Faith always has something to say. Jesus put it this way:
Mark 11:

22   So Jesus answered and said to them, "Have faith in God.
23   For assuredly, I say to you, whoever says to this mountain, 'Be removed and be cast into the sea,' and does not doubt in his heart, but believes that those things he says will be done, he will have whatever he says.

Someone said that you have to say a thing three times as much as you believe it. You can locate a person's spiritual level by their conversation. You can listen to a person speak and recognize how spiritual they are, what they believe and how much they believe it.

People usually say in conversation what they really think or believe. It is no use praying for a healing and saying you probably won't get it. Listen to the conversation of non-believers or even 'unbelieving believers' and you will hear a lot of cynicism and negativity. A lot of people just say that they don't expect things to work out for them. That's what they say, what they believe and what they receive.

Proverbs 18:21:

Death and life are in the power of the tongue,
And those who love it will eat its fruit.

You can hear thoughts of loss, grief or even death in the words of many songs. Perhaps that's the reason that so many musicians tragically die young. So be careful that you're not being killed softly by someone's song.

If we are going to get serious about pleasing God, and then receiving from God, we need to make sure our words line up with what we're believing for.

Faith is always believing for something. It may not have manifested yet but the person of faith is always believing and confessing what they believe. When our words are consistent with our prayers and believing, then God can get involved and the answer and manifestation to our prayers is on the way.

Our confession of faith plays a vital role in our victory over Satan. And this is why he has fought this teaching so much, even using sections of the church to attack the teaching.

Revelation 12:11:

And they overcame him [Satan] by the blood of the Lamb and by the word of their testimony,

Satan knows that when believers are bold in their faith, and in their confession of the Word of God, they can't be defeated and he will be the loser.

Faith for when Jesus Returns

God has a plan of redemption for humankind, and He has given us responsibility for making it happen. He is working to a timetable. We, the body of Christ, are his agents on the earth and are tasked with sharing the Good News of redemption through Jesus with the world.

We need to believe for His enabling power to be able to complete the task. We need to learn how to believe God for the humanly impossible. We need to learn how to operate on this earth as Jesus taught us to by believing His Word; His promises that belong to us by covenant.

1 Timothy 6:12:

> Fight the good fight of faith, lay hold on eternal life, to which you were also called and have confessed the good confession in the presence of many witnesses.

The devil is attacking our faith in any way he can. He wants to get us into doubt so we won't receive anything from God, even the forgiveness that has already been paid for. When Jesus returns to gather His people to be with Him forever, He will be looking for faith.

Luke 18:8:

> … Nevertheless, when the Son of Man comes, will He really find faith on the earth?

Praise God, if Jesus returns in our lifetime, He'll find faith in us.

IV
The Doctrine of Baptisms

The word *baptism* (Vines p. 96) means 'immersion, submersion and emergence'. The Greeks of the New Testament era used the word to describe dipping a garment or cloth into a dye to change its color. So, when the Bible talks about baptism it is talking about being immersed into something or someone and being changed by the experience.

Notice the term 'the doctrines of baptisms' (Hebrews 6:2) is plural. The writer of Hebrews tells us that the early church believed in more than one baptism. The first form of baptism we are usually familiar with is the baptism of repentance by John the Baptist; however, this really belonged to the Old Covenant and was not practiced by the early church.

I believe the Bible teaches that there are three baptisms that apply to the New Covenant believer:

1. What is sometimes called the Christian baptism.
2. Water baptism.
3. The baptism with the Holy Spirit.

The Christian Baptism

The Christian baptism is the experience of immersion into the family of God when a person chooses to believe in Jesus as their personal savior. The Bible also talks of this as being 'born again'.

John 3:3

> ... Most assuredly, I say to you, unless one is born again, he cannot see the Kingdom of God.

It has also been called the 'new birth'. A person's body is alive, even though they are spiritually dead, until their spirit is made alive to the things of God. When a person believes in Jesus, they are made right with God and have the right to live with Him forever. They are born for the second time, this time spiritually.

For a person to enter the kingdom of God they must first of all be born into this world. The term 'born of water' could refer to the fact that when a baby is born the mother's waters break. The natural process for any baby to be born into the world is for the fluid around the baby in the womb to be expelled just prior to delivery. Therefore, the delivery of any baby into the physical world involves being 'born of water'.

Likewise, to be born again we must be born spiritually through the work of the Holy Spirit. God the Holy Spirit does a work of regeneration, making our spirit alive to the relationship with the Father, Son and Himself. This is something we cannot do for ourselves; it is done for us by God.

Michael McKeon

1 Corinthians 12:13:

For by one Spirit we were all baptized into one body – whether Jews or Greeks, whether slaves or free – and have all been made to drink into one Spirit.

Here we are told that when we became believers we were baptized into 'one body'; the body of Christ by the Spirit. This is our Christian baptism; we are immersed into one spiritual body made up of many individuals completing a unified body with Jesus at the head. This is accomplished by the Holy Spirit, not by ourselves, not by the church or even by Jesus. The Holy Spirit baptizes us into the body of Christ.

The book of Hebrews talks about baptism as being plural, that there are more than one, and yet why do other passages of scripture refer to 'baptism', singular? This is why God places teachers in the church, because these things need to be taught and explained by people gifted in this way. The believers need to be diligent about seeking understanding about God's Word, especially from anointed teachers, so that they can explain things or "rightly divide the word of truth" (2 Timothy 2:15). It is possible to misunderstand the scriptures; therefore, we need the help God has placed in the church so that we can believe what God intended and live in victory.

Ephesians 4:

4 There is one body and one Spirit, just as you were called in one hope of your calling;
5 one Lord, one faith, one baptism;

These passages are talking about one particular type of baptism – the Christian baptism. It is talking about the baptism whereby we are saved. There is only one body of believers and one Holy Spirit who will baptize or immerse a person into the body of believers; the family of God.

From the time a person believes in Jesus and is saved, they actually have the Holy Spirit in them, but they are not baptized or filled with the Holy Spirit yet. The baptism of the Holy Spirit is a separate event in the life of the believer.

Romans 8:11

> But if the Spirit of Him who raised Jesus from the dead dwells in you, He who raised Christ from the dead will also give life to your mortal bodies through His Spirit who dwells in you.

If we look at what Jesus said to the disciples after His resurrection in John 20:22:

> … He breathed on them, and said to them, "Receive the Holy Spirit."

Jesus breathed on His disciples and imparted the new life of the New Covenant.

This event confirmed their redemption and the beginning of the New Covenant. They were not overflowing with spiritual power until the day of Pentecost when they were baptized and filled with the Holy Spirit.

Once a person is born again, spiritually they become a new creation. The Bible also expresses this as being "in Him", "in Whom" or "in Christ" approximately 140 times in the New Testament. This expression "being in Him" or "in Christ" is consistent with the notion of baptism or being immersed into

Jesus. It goes deep and the truth of it needs to be revealed to us rather than understood with our minds. I believe that the experience of Noah and his family being inside the Ark is a type of being "in Him" or "in Christ". Outside the Ark, God was judging and destroying the world by flood; inside there was safety and deliverance. Likewise, New Testament believers are "in Him", "in Whom" and "in Christ" and are saved from the judgment and spiritual death that is outside fellowship with Him.

2 Corinthians 5:

17   Therefore, if anyone is in Christ, he is a new creation; old things have passed away; behold, all things have become new.
21   For He made Him who knew no sin to be sin for us, that we might become the righteousness of God in Him.

Physically, a new believer looks the same and sounds the same, but they will start to behave differently. They now have a nature from their Father in heaven and have started the process of shedding their sinful nature. They are having a change of heart.

Any person who chooses to believe in Jesus has had their past sins taken away, and they are made as spiritually new and pure as a newborn spiritual baby. They still have a lot of spiritual growing to do, the devil will still attack them but they are born into the family of God with all the rights and privileges of God's son or a daughter.

This is our Christian baptism. We are immersed into the family and life of God. Until we are born again we are not in a right relationship with God.

A Spiritual Foundation for Christians

1 Thessalonians 5:23

Now may the God of peace Himself sanctify you completely; and may your whole spirit, soul, and body be preserved blameless at the coming of our Lord Jesus Christ.

Human beings are made up of an eternal spirit, a soul or a soulishness and a physical body. Usually, we are more conscious of our bodies than our eternal spirit. The soul is more difficult to define. The soul is the will, the mind and the emotions. It is that part of us that says I will or I won't. It is the self or the ego. It is the part of us that says yes or no to God.

Infant baptism, which involves pouring water over a baby's head, and is practiced in some denominations, does not make a person right with God. It was not taught or practiced in the New Testament church.

The Jews had a dedication ceremony for infants but it wasn't baptism. Jewish children were not considered responsible for their own significant moral choices until the age of twelve. They were under the responsibility of an adult, normally the parent, to guide them in learning God's ways of doing things. However, from the age of twelve they were expected to bear the responsibility for their actions themselves. I believe there is a lot to be said for this approach to the age of moral decision-making and personal responsibility.

If an infant or young child dies before the age of twelve, I believe God is merciful and just and that child will go to be with the Lord enjoying His presence forever more. However, those adults – even young adults – who hear the Good News of the kingdom and reject God who is Love, have made a very poor choice.

Michael McKeon

Men and women are the high point of God's creation. God created humankind to relate with, to love and enjoy our company as a father enjoys the company of his children. The Bible says we are created in His image and likeness, which is the ultimate source of our human rights (Genesis 1:27). This is why we have self-worth and the right to be treated justly. We are created in the God class with a spirit that can communicate with Him. We can make choices and God respects our choices.

He will not force us to believe Him and come into a right relationship with Him. He leaves that up to us. He will abide by our choice for all eternity, though not without the pain of separation on His part on the day of judgment.

Our Christian baptism brings us into a right relationship with God where we can inherit all the promises in His Word and then enter into eternal life with Him. King David made many mistakes but he always turned back to God because he knew in his heart of hearts that the benefits of a right relationship with God by far exceeded the attraction of sin.

Psalm 16:11

You will show me the path of life;
In Your presence is fullness of joy;
At Your right hand are pleasures forevermore.

If you don't know whether you're saved and are going to spend eternity with the God who is Love, it is easy to gain a certainty from a promise in the Bible. This promise is a very effective passage to use when witnessing to someone to help bring them to a decision about believing in Jesus and being born again. It's not about joining a particular church. It's about believing what God said and doing what He asks.

Every believer should know Romans 10:9

> that if you confess with your mouth the Lord Jesus and believe in your heart that God has raised Him from the dead, you will be saved.

This scripture provides a simple and absolute promise from God of what to say and believe in order to receive the Christian baptism and begin the life that will lead them to enjoy 'the fullness of joy' with Him forever.

Water Baptism

Jesus commanded water baptism
   Mark 16:16

> He who believes and is baptized will be saved; but he who does not believe will be condemned.

Notice from this scripture that it is the person who believes, and, in the natural course of events, is baptized, who will be saved. The condemnation depends on whether they believed, not on whether they were baptized. Clearly, receiving redemption does not depend exclusively on whether they have been fully immersed in water. It depends on whether a person believes.
   It was the usual practice in the early church for believers to be fully immersed in water. Water baptism usually occurred immediately after the decision to believe in and confess Jesus as Lord and savior. This is not always the practice today, but it is the preferred time for the baptism to occur.

When Peter was filled with the Holy Spirit on the day of Pentecost, he said;
Acts 2:38;

Repent, and let every one of you be baptized in the name of Jesus Christ for the remission of sins; and you shall receive the gift of the Holy Spirit.

In Acts 8:26–40, Phillip was sent by an angel to minister to a eunuch, who was the treasurer to the queen of Ethiopians. This man was studying Isaiah 53 when Phillip arrived and explained that the passage was about Jesus. The eunuch believed and asked to be baptized immediately:
Acts 8:

36   ... See, here is water. What hinders me from being baptized?
37   Then Phillip said, "If you believe with all your heart, you may." And he answered and said, "I believe that Jesus Christ is the Son of God."
38   So he commanded the chariot to stand still. And both Phillip and the eunuch went down into the water, and he baptized him.

Jesus commanded water baptism and it was the practice of the church.

Infant baptism is not the same as water baptism. Infant baptism does not involve the choice of the infant involved, and does not constitute belief in Jesus by that infant. It was not taught or practiced in the New Testament church.

Adult water baptism is a deeply symbolic and supernatural experience. It is symbolic in that it stands for the death, burial and resurrection of Jesus. It is also an actual spiritual experience that causes certain things to happen in a person's life.

A rite of passage

Water baptism is a rite of passage in the life of the believer, and is an experience the believer will never forget. It is an act of obedience on the part of the believer, and a statement to the church and the world that this person identifies with the death, burial and resurrection of Jesus. This pleases God.

Romans 6:

4   Therefore we were buried with Him through baptism into death, that just as Christ was raised from the dead by the glory of the Father, even so we also should walk in newness of life.
5   For if we have been united together in the likeness of His death, certainly we also shall be in the likeness of His resurrection,

Just as Jesus died and went into the grave, this believer goes into the water to identify with what Jesus did on our behalf. Likewise, as Jesus the anointed savior rose from the dead and came out of the tomb, the believer rises up out of the water. Jesus did that not only for Himself but as "the firstborn from the dead" (Colossians 1:18). If Jesus was the firstborn from the dead, then there are others. God is still counting and you and I have a number too. Isn't that amazing! God has always known the day of our birth, death and resurrection. He has us on His mind and in His heart and He is counting down the days when we will see Him face to face. We should live with a strong consciousness of that fact. That way we will live our lives with the right priorities.

If we identify with the death of Jesus and the appeasing sacrifice of His blood to pay for our sins, then we will physically rise from the dead in the same manner as He did. Jesus has paid the ransom for your life and mine.

Remission of sins

Peter associated the remission (forgiveness) of sins with water baptism. In his sermon on the day of Pentecost he called on everyone who heard him to repent and be baptized. The scripture doesn't specifically say water baptism but on consideration I think Peter means water baptism. Three thousand people in Jerusalem that day obeyed and were baptized.

Acts 2:38:

> … Repent, and let every one of you be baptized in the name of Jesus Christ for the remission of sins;

It is true that all the sins committed before a person believes in Jesus are wiped away at the time they are born again. It is not necessary for a person to confess every single sin when they believe and receive their Christian baptism; God knows it all. Other people's sins are no one else's business. God wants to hear a confession of faith in Jesus as Lord and God, and sin in general and the record of all sins is paid for and blotted out.

A spiritual circumcision

In the Old Covenant, God told Abraham to circumcise all the males as a sign of the covenant (Genesis 17:10–11). The physical circumcision of the foreskin as a sign of a covenant with God is a remarkable thing. It is very personal; it is made for life and the man who is so marked can never forget it. Circumcision changes things.

Physical circumcision of the old covenant was something that God used in the New Covenant to portray circumcision of the heart. Colossians 2:

> 11   In Him you were also circumcised with the circumcision made without hands, by putting off the body of the sins of the flesh, by the circumcision of Christ,
> 12   buried with Him in baptism, in which you were also raised with Him through faith in the working of God, who raised Him from the dead.

Our hearts are forever changed when we believe and are baptized. Paul received this revelation that God does a work in our lives that we couldn't achieve by ourselves. We just don't have that ability.

"In Him you were also circumcised" (verse 11) shows that when a person believes in Jesus they receive a circumcision of the heart, not of the flesh and don't need to be circumcised physically. The sign of their covenant is written in their heart.

"…by putting off the body of the sins of the flesh" (verse 11) means that before baptism our hearts were oriented away from God and toward sin. After baptism, our hearts are oriented toward God and away from sin. We will tend to resist sin as we start to see it the way God does. We are now in a relationship with Him, and as we fellowship with Him we become more like Him.

God wanted to build on the Old Testament sign of the covenant and transcend that to a better sign that was not merely external but also spiritual. The original physical circumcision was always meant to point toward spiritual circumcision of the heart.

1 Peter 3:21

> There is also an antitype which now saves us – baptism (not the removal of the filth of the flesh, but the answer of a good conscience toward God), through the resurrection of Jesus Christ,

Where once God destroyed life through the flood of water, now it is the opposite, He will save everyone who is immersed in water in obedience and faith. Water baptism is a confirmation of salvation. It should be part and parcel of the salvation process of belief, confession and then baptism. If a believer has never been water baptized, there is unfinished business in their life. They are saved but God would like them to complete the process.

Baptism with the Holy Spirit

In the Old Testament there were only certain people that God chose to fill with His Holy Spirit. It was a privilege that was only available to a select small number of people. These people had a special assignment that needed a special ability to be able to carry it out, and God empowered them with His Spirit to do that. I've only been able to find eleven instances when God filled people with His Spirit in the Old Testament.

A Spiritual Foundation for Christians

1. One of these was a man named Bezalel. He was chosen by God to oversee the work of building and crafting everything that would be involved in worship: the tabernacle of meeting, the ark of the testimony and the mercy seat that is on it, and all the furniture of the tabernacle, the gold lampstand and the altars, and the garments that the priest wore (Exodus 31:1–11).

Exodus 31:3

> And I have filled Him with the Spirit of God, in wisdom, in understanding, in knowledge, and in all manner of workmanship,

2 & 3. Moses and 70 elders had or were filled with the Holy Spirit to perform their ministry. Moses had been micromanaging the whole population. God had let him go on like this until he asked for help. Then God gave Moses the solution. He would anoint and empower seventy elders of the people with His Spirit as He had done to Moses. So, God provided seventy anointed leaders to help with the task of managing the children of Israel, who were being turned into a nation.

Numbers 11:17

> Then I will come down and talk with you there. I will take of the Spirit that is upon you and will put the same upon them; and they shall bear the burden of the people with you, that you may not bear it yourself alone.

4. When God told Moses that he was about to die, He said it this way. He was going to be "gathered to his people" (Numbers 27:13). Being the leader that he was, Moses' first thought was to ask God to provide another leader for the people. God replied and told him that He already had someone, who had His Spirit in him.

Numbers 27:18

And the Lord said to Moses: "Take Joshua the son of Nun with you, a man in whom is the Spirit, and lay your hand on him;

5. Samson was also filled with the Holy Spirit. He was anointed to deliver Israel through physical strength. He was probably about average in size but what made the difference was the empowering of the Holy Spirit.

Judges 13:25

And the Spirit of the Lord began to move upon him at Mahaneh Dan between Zorah and Eshtaol.

6. Saul was transformed by the Holy Spirit when he was anointed king. The Word doesn't say that he was filled with the Holy Spirit, but this is what happened to Saul after Samuel prophesied.

1 Samuel 10:6

> Then the Spirit of the Lord will come upon you, and you will prophesy with them and be turned into another man.

Saul was anointed and empowered to be king. God didn't want a king but the people insisted. God decided that if they had to have a king he had to have the ability to do the job. Saul was God's choice and he was a good leader for a time but Saul's character let him down. It is still the same today with some of God's people; they can be highly anointed but if they compromise their faithfulness to God, they'll fall.

7. After the Lord rejected Saul from being king, He chose David and filled him with His Spirit. A good king needs a high degree of skills and abilities to be effective. They face many risks and opportunities and it takes an anointed leader to guide the nation on the path God has set.

1 Samuel 16:13:

> Then Samuel took the horn of oil and anointed him in the midst of his brothers; and the Spirit of the Lord came upon David from that day forward.

8. & 9. When Mary the mother of Jesus went to visit her cousin Elizabeth, who was the mother of John the Baptist, Elizabeth was filled with the Holy Spirit. It could be

that John was filled with or baptized with the Holy Spirit in his mother's womb.

Luke 1:41

And it happened, when Elizabeth heard the greeting of Mary, that the babe leaped in her womb; and Elizabeth was filled with the Holy Spirit.

After being filled with the Holy Spirit, Elizabeth prophesied (Luke 1:42–45). She was given a revelation from heaven and spoke it out. She didn't have that ability before being filled with the Holy Spirit. That's how it was with everyone in the Bible accounts. Once they were filled with or baptized into the Holy Spirit, they were given a supernatural ability to do whatever they were called to do.

10. After Zacharias announced his son's name as john Luke's gospel records that he was filled with the Holy Spirit.

Luke 1:67

Now his father Zacharias was filled with the Holy Spirit and prophesied.

11. The Holy Spirit "was upon" Simeon in Luke's gospel and it could be that he was filled with the Holy Spirit. There are three references to the Holy Spirit in three consecutive verses concerning Simeon's presence at the time when Mary and Joseph brought Jesus to the temple after his birth to present Him to God His father. Luke 2:25-27

And that is how it is for us today. Under the new covenant the same Holy Spirit will empower or anoint all believers to minister, especially in the gifts of the Holy Spirit, "for the profit of all" (1 Corinthians 12:7). The charismatic gifts are given after a believer has been baptized with the Holy Spirit. The gifts are for the benefit of everyone and are not meant exclusively for the recipient of the gift. All believers need the Holy Spirit to be better able to receive from God and be a more effective witness.

Acts 1:8:

> But you shall receive power when the Holy Spirit has come upon you; and you shall be witnesses to Me in Jerusalem, and in all Judea and Samaria, and to the end of the earth."

If we are to make disciples of all nations, we need the ability of the Holy Spirit to overcome everything the devil throws at us. Many Christians have worked hard and used their talents to the best of their abilities and achieved some great successes for the Lord. Praise God for that. Think what could have been done if they had been Holy Spirit-empowered operating in the gifts of Holy Spirit. Jesus told the disciples not to leave Jerusalem until they had received the power of the Holy Spirit.

Luke 24:49:

> Behold, I send the Promise of My Father upon you; but tarry in the city of Jerusalem until you are endued with power from on high."

Believers also need the infilling of the Holy Spirit to help live a victorious Christian life. It is not only ministers that need the anointing; all believers need the empowering of the Holy Spirit to enable them to live their lives in holiness. The Holy Spirit can help a person perform their work with an ability that looks as though it just comes 'naturally' but, really, it comes supernaturally. Parents need the wisdom of the Holy Spirit to raise children, and some children need the wisdom of the Holy Spirit to minister to their parents.

When I was filled with the Holy Spirit, I didn't feel anything. I didn't prophesy. All I could do was make a single-syllable sound. Some people call that baby tongues because it sounds like a baby when they are starting to talk.

I was told to speak out the sound that the Holy Spirit gave me. I was making this single sound over and over again. As I practiced my prayer language, I became more fluent.

I had been believing to receive the Holy Spirit for a long time, and when I did there was no great manifestation, it just happened quietly. Everyone is different and the Holy Spirit deals with us in different ways.

There was also the baptism of John. John the Baptist, the son of Elizabeth, was the cousin of Jesus and baptized people in the Jordan River. He witnessed to the baptism of the Holy Spirit.

His message and his baptism were for repentance. The people came to John to hear a message from a prophet. The last prophet in Israel was Malachi, who had ministered some 400 years earlier. As he preached, people came from far and wide and repented. There was a revival happening in a remote place with an unlikely figure dressed in camel hair and living off the land. People repented in their hearts and as a sign of their repentance, their turning away from sin, they were baptized by John in the Jordan River.

He was a prophet who was to "Prepare the way of the Lord" (Isaiah 40:3). He was anointed to prepare the way for the ministry of Jesus, the Lamb of God who would take away the sin of the world (John 1:29).

John's baptism was based on a purification rite of his time. It was a ceremony and symbolism that people understood. John's baptism of repentance in the waters of the Jordan River symbolized the true purifying that was coming with the Lamb of God. John prophesied that the baptism Jesus offers is an immersion into the life and holiness of God. The fire of God's Holy Spirit will burn up the pollution of sin and unfaithfulness to God. This will create a church with a pure heart and not just an outward compliance.

John 1

25 And they asked him, saying, "Why then do you baptize if you are not the Christ, nor Elijah, nor the Prophet?"
26 John answered them, saying, "I baptize with water, but there stands One among you whom you do not know.
27 "It is He who, coming after me, is preferred before me, whose sandal strap I am not worthy to loose."
28 These things were done in Bethabara beyond the Jordan, where John was baptizing.
29 The next day John saw Jesus coming toward him, and said, "Behold! The Lamb of God who takes away the sin of the world!
30 This is He of whom I said, 'After me comes a Man who is preferred before me, for He was before me.'
31 I did not know Him, but that He should be revealed to Israel, therefore I came baptizing with water."

> 32 And John bore witness, saying, "I saw the Spirit descending from heaven like a dove, and He remained upon Him.
> 33 I did not know Him, but He who sent me to baptize with water said to me, 'Upon whom you see the Spirit descending, and remaining on Him, this is He who baptizes with the Holy Spirit.'
> 34 And I have seen and testified that this is the Son of God."

In verse 33 we see two baptisms mentioned; baptism with water and baptism with the Holy Spirit. John would carry out the baptism with water, so who would carry out the baptism with the Holy Spirit? Not all believers are aware of this other ministry of Jesus; baptizing with the Holy Spirit. This is something Jesus does to this day, just as He continues in His primary ministry of taking away the sin of the world. People keep sinning and the blood of Jesus is still effective in paying the price for sin.

We don't doubt that when Jesus said, "It is finished!", in John 19:30, that the payment for the sin of the world was complete. We shouldn't doubt that the other part of His ministry – baptizing with the Holy Spirit – is still being performed while there are believers on earth.

Anyone who reads the gospels realizes that although there is a common theme between each gospel, there are also different emphases given by each writer. They each had a different audience and a different priority as they wrote their account of Jesus' life and message. Sometimes the same story can be told with different detail, which can be surprising; for example, the resurrection of Jesus. However, when I first studied the baptism of the Holy Spirit, it blessed me to read that each of the gospel writers recorded the ministry of Jesus in baptizing the believer with the Holy Spirit.

This wasn't a priority for just one writer, it was recorded in all four gospels and it is still a priority for Jesus. Being filled with the Holy Spirit should be a priority for all believers if they haven't already received from that part of Jesus' ministry. Why receive from one part of the ministry but not the other? This is the ministry of Jesus; I think we should accept all of it. He has gone to a lot of trouble to make it available. I'm sure it would please the Father, Jesus and the Holy Spirit if all the church would accept Jesus' entire ministry.

Matthew 3:11

> I indeed baptize you with water unto repentance, but He who is coming after me is mightier than I, whose sandals I am not worthy to carry. He will baptize you with the Holy Spirit and fire.

Mark 1:8:

> I indeed baptize you with water, but He will baptize you with the Holy Spirit.

Luke 3:16:

> John answered, saying to all, "I indeed baptize you with water; but One mightier than I is coming, whose sandal strap I am not worthy to loose. He will baptize you with the Holy Spirit and fire.

The baptism with the Holy Spirit is something only available to believers. Unbelievers cannot receive the Holy Spirit. This is shown in the passage below.

John 14:

16 And I will pray the Father, and He will give you another Helper, that He may abide with you forever –
17 the Spirit of truth whom the world cannot receive, because it neither sees Him nor knows Him; but you know Him, for He dwells with you and will be in you.

The term "the world" in verse 17 refers to unbelievers. Anyone who hasn't accepted Jesus as Lord and Savior cannot be baptized with the Holy Spirit. They are not eligible to receive. You need to be a believer first, and then you may receive. This is what Jesus taught. If unbelievers are being empowered by any kind of spirit, it is not the Holy Spirit.

The promise that all believers could be filled with the Holy Spirit was prophesied by Joel, and was fulfilled on the day of Pentecost.

Joel 2:

28 And it shall come to pass afterward that I will pour out My Spirit on all flesh; your sons and your daughters shall prophesy, your old men shall dream dreams, your young men shall see visions.
29 And also on My menservants and on My maidservants I will pour out My Spirit in those days.

Pentecost is a Greek word and means the fiftieth day after Passover. To the Jews it was known as the Feast of Weeks, being seven weeks with the feast day being the next day, making fifty days after Passover (Deuteronomy 16:9–12). It also celebrated the wheat harvest, which was an event of national importance.

Numbers 28:26:

> Also on the day of the first fruits when you bring a new grain offering to the Lord at your Feast of Weeks, you shall have a holy convocation. You shall do no customary work.

The Feast of Harvest occurred in the third month of the Hebrew calendar (May–June), and celebrated the early harvest and was a type of Pentecost. This was the first great harvest of believers to receive the baptism with Holy Spirit. The Feast of Ingathering, or Tabernacles (Booths), occurred from September to October. This was an autumn feast that honored God for the completed harvest and occurred in the seventh Hebrew month. This Feast of Tabernacles will also see a fulfillment under the New Covenant as a great ingathering of people to the family of God.

God initiated these feasts and gave them to the Old Covenant community, the nation of Israel, to observe. Then He built on the meaning of the original ceremonies and completed their significance. The New Covenant community, the church or spiritual Israel, was filled with the Holy Spirit and became the first fruits. It could be argued that the New Testament church was born that day. God the Holy Spirit filled the believers gathered in the upper room, and the first fruit of Spirit-filled believers went out and witnessed with anointing to the world. This first outpouring of the Holy Spirit led to 3,000 salvations on the first day.

Acts 2:

1. When the Day of Pentecost had fully come, they were all with one accord in one place.
2. And suddenly there came a sound from heaven, as of a rushing mighty wind, and it filled the whole house where they were sitting.
3. Then there appeared to them divided tongues, as of fire, and one sat upon each of them.
4. And they were all filled with the Holy Spirit and began to speak with other tongues, as the Spirit gave them utterance.

Notice it says, "When the Day of Pentecost had fully come" – God had been waiting for this day since the beginning of creation. He had been waiting for the early harvest. This was a great day in the history of redemption. This was the first fruits of a harvest that is going to continue right up to the latter harvest, when Jesus returns to collect the church.

The Holy Spirit manifested as "a rushing mighty wind" and "tongues as of fire". The Holy Spirit is a person, the third person of the Trinity, and can manifest in any way He chooses. Sometimes He has an effect on people that is surprising and not very 'religious'. People laugh, they cry, they can fall over and talk in a language that He gives (verse 4). He has a way of knocking people off their high religious horses. He'll do a lot more than that if we cooperate with Him and be open to His gifts (1 Corinthians 12).

A Spiritual Foundation for Christians

For the first ten years, the disciples ministered almost exclusively among the Jews. They thought they were doing what God wanted by just leading Jewish people to Jesus. They hadn't seen themselves ministering beyond the borders of Israel or to people of other races.

God had other plans. God gave Peter, who was the leader of the early church, a vision and an experience that he couldn't deny was a revelation from God about the universality of God's plan for redemption and baptism with the Holy Spirit.

There was a Roman soldier, Cornelius, who was a centurion with the army. The Bible says he was devout, feared God, gave generously and prayed always. He had a heart for God. I think any pastor would want to have more people like Cornelius come to their church. God gave him a vision and told him to send for Simon Peter. Then God gave Peter a vision. He was not to call God's creatures unclean when He had made them clean. Then the men arrived and took Peter to Cornelius. Peter realized that he couldn't look down on and ignore these people from another country who were not Jewish, and started ministering to the household.

Acts 10:

44 While Peter was still speaking these words, the Holy Spirit fell upon all those who heard the word.
45 And those of the circumcision who believed were astonished, as many as came with Peter, because the gift of the Holy Spirit had been poured out on the Gentiles also.
46 For they heard them speak with tongues and magnify God. Then Peter answered,

47 "Can anyone forbid water, that these should not be baptized who have received the Holy Spirit just as we have?"
48 And he commanded them to be baptized in the name of the Lord.

These people believed in Jesus while Peter shared with them, and they were baptized into the Holy Spirit by Jesus at that time. Peter wanted to complete the process and have them water baptized straightaway. He was satisfied that they were entitled to the full benefits of Jesus' ministry and that God had given them equal status in His kingdom. Peter was teachable; when he was shown he was wrong he would change his opinion.

It is generally considered that twenty years after the resurrection of Jesus the following episode in Acts 19 occurred. When the Apostle Paul came to Ephesus, he met some people who were disciples. He talked with them and discovered that they had not even heard of the Holy Spirit let alone the baptism with the Holy Spirit. He was very surprised because it was normal for believers in Jesus in the first-century church to be filled with the Holy Spirit. Immediately, Paul asked about what baptism they had received? This would tell what kind of believers they were. When they said they had received John's baptism he understood that they had not received the baptism of salvation or the baptism with the Holy Spirit.

Acts 19:

1 And it happened, while Apollos was at Corinth, that Paul, having passed through the upper regions came to Ephesus. And finding some disciples

2 he said to them, "Did you receive the Holy Spirit when you believed?" So they said to him, "We have not so much as heard whether there is a Holy Spirit."
3 And he said to them, "Into what then were you baptized?" So they said, "Into John's Baptism."
4 Then Paul said, "John indeed baptized with a baptism of repentance, saying to the people that they should believe on Him who would come after him, that is, on Christ Jesus."
5 When they heard this, they were baptized in the name of the Lord Jesus.
6 And when Paul had laid hands on them, the Holy Spirit came upon them, and they spoke with tongues and prophesied.
7 Now the men were about twelve in all.

These twelve men listened to Paul and believed his message. They were baptized into "the name of the Lord Jesus" (verse 5). To the writers of the Bible, the name of a person stands for their nature. So when someone is baptized into the "name of the Lord Jesus", they are immersed into the nature of Jesus, the Lord of Lords and King of Kings.

Paul then laid hands on them to receive or be filled with the Holy Spirit. They received immediately.

It's important to notice that in each of the New Testament accounts when a believer is baptized with the Holy Spirit, they start saying something. To speak in tongues means to speak in a language given by God. Sometimes it is actually a language spoken somewhere in the world, but commonly it is a heavenly language imparted by the Holy Spirit to communicate directly from the human spirit to God. Revelation can be received from God as to the meaning of the communication.

In Acts 2:4, on the day of Pentecost:

> And they were all filled with the Holy Spirit and began to speak with other tongues, as the Spirit gave them utterance.

In Acts 10:46, when Cornelius' family and servants received the Holy Spirit, they spoke out what the Holy Spirit gave them: "For they heard them speak with tongues and magnify God."

In Acts 19:6, the twelve men in Ephesus "spoke with tongues and prophesied".

The book of Acts gives a consistent record that when believers were baptized with the Holy Spirit they started speaking in tongues and sometimes prophesied. Speaking in tongues was seen as evidence by the early church that believers had been filled with the Holy Spirit. It was evidence then and I believe it is still evidence today.

The terminology used to describe the experience is fluid. It is the language of a relationship with the Holy Spirit. The Bible talks about being baptized with, or immersed into (John 1:33), or being filled with (Acts 2:4), the Holy Spirit. Paul also used the expression "receive the Holy Spirit" (Acts 19:2) to describe the experience. Another expression is "the Holy Spirit came upon them" (Acts 19:6).

Before I was baptized with the Holy Spirit, I knew the gospels and the story of the book of Acts, but reading the Bible was like reading a mathematics textbook. I could read the words but I couldn't put it together. I had studied the Bible before but it had been largely a theoretical exercise that didn't build faith.

After I was baptized with the Holy Spirit, I started to notice that I could more easily relate to Jesus as a person, and the Word of God became more meaningful to me. Now I was on the right path and I began to discern teaching and a greater meaning in the Word of God that would feed my spirit.

This is a spiritual experience and if anyone is truly searching for God this is the relationship and experience they need. The baptism with the Holy Spirit is the key to the deeper things of God that satisfy the searching heart.

The following table summarizes the Bible's teaching on baptisms.

Type of Baptism	Type of Person	The Baptizer	Baptized With/Into
Christian	Sinner	Holy Spirit	Body of Christ
Water	Believer	The Church	Body of Christ
Holy Spirit	Believer	Jesus	Holy Spirit

V
Laying on of Hands

Laying on of hands is one way of accessing God's supernatural power. It is a Biblical practice to lay hands on someone and it was used throughout the Bible for three reasons:

1. To impart or transfer something from one to another.
2. To Identify or bond with.
3. Dedication or commission.

Throughout the Bible, God uses the laying on of hands to achieve a number of vitally important results.

Old Testament Atonement for Sin

In the Old Testament, hands were laid on animal sacrifices to transfer sin from the guilty to the innocent. God chose the laying on of hands as the practice to achieve this.

Leviticus 1:4

Then he shall put his hand on the head of the burnt offering, and it will be accepted on his behalf to make atonement for him.

In the case of the whole burnt offering, any man could bring a bull to the door of the tabernacle and lay his hand on the bull as a means to transfer the sin and the guilt of his household to the bull. In this way, the bull would be identified with the sin and pay the price for it. Every man in Israel was eligible to participate in this means of atonement. As men participated in the whole burnt offering throughout their lives, it taught them an unforgettable lesson in that sin could be transferred from the guilty to the innocent, thereby setting them free.

On the Day of Atonement, the corporate sin of the people of Israel was transferred.

Leviticus 16

21 Aaron shall lay both his hands on the head of the live goat, confess over it all the iniquities of the children of Israel, and all their transgressions concerning all their sins, putting them on the head of the goat, and shall send it away into the wilderness by the hand of a suitable man.
22 The goat shall bear on itself all their iniquities to an uninhabited land; and he shall release the goat in the wilderness.

Aaron laid both his hands on the head of the goat and confessed the sins of the people over the goat. Those sins were passed on to the goat and the goat bore "on itself" the iniquities of the people of Israel. The scapegoat was led so far away into the wilderness that it never returned. By using this experience, God was saying that when He forgave sin it never returned; the scapegoat carried it away. God doesn't even remember sin when it's been forgiven.

This type of atonement for sin provided one year's grace. The people's sins were covered in this way by the sacrifice of the innocent for the guilty each year. It was also symbolic, pointing to the real scapegoat, Jesus, who came later carrying our sin away once and for all.

The Baptism with the Holy Spirit

The laying on of hands was also used in the baptism with the Holy Spirit. The usual means by which people were baptized with the Holy Spirit in the New Testament is by the laying on of hands. However, this is not the only means by which people were and may still be baptized with the Holy Spirit. There were two occasions recorded in Acts when God intervened and filled people with the Holy Spirit without human hands being laid on anyone. The first time was on the day of Pentecost in Acts 2, and the second instance recorded in the New Testament was with Cornelius' household in Acts 10.

As we noted in the last chapter, God baptized a number of people in the Old Testament with the Holy Spirit at His own choosing. That shouldn't surprise us because the great plan and sacrifice for our redemption is initiated and paid for by God. God has always done surprising things in the past and I am sure he will continue to do so.

There are three clear and specific examples of believers receiving the Holy Spirit through the laying on of hands in the New Testament.

First in Acts 8, Phillip traveled to Samaria and preached the Word. In verse 5 it says he "preached Christ to them". Remember, the word Christ isn't Jesus' last name, it is a title. The Greek word *Christ* (Strong's #5547) and the Hebrew word *Messiah* (Strong's #4899) both mean anointed and consecrated. It carries with it the understanding that the person is empowered by God to fulfill their calling. In the Old Testament, this was usually the king or priest, but in the New Testament, all believers can be anointed by the Holy Spirit to fulfill their particular ministry.

This verse in Acts could be translated, "Phillip preached the Anointed and His anointing to them." If you are preaching about the Anointed and His anointing, it follows that people are going to want to receive the anointing of the Holy Spirit, as well as the Anointed, Jesus. It was, after all, the anointing that empowered Jesus to fulfill His calling as the Christ or Messiah.

Acts 8

17   Then they laid hands on them, and they received the Holy Spirit,
18   And when Simon saw that through the laying on of the apostles' hands the Holy Spirit was given, he offered them money,

The whole world, including Simon the sorcerer, could see that the Holy Spirit was imparted by the laying on of hands. He was only interested in the 'power' or anointing and wanted to pay for it, but you can't buy God.

Secondly In Acts, chapter 9, Saul received the baptism of the Holy Spirit through the laying on of Ananias' hands. This is the only reference we have of this second Ananias in the New Testament. It is his only recorded act, but it was a courageous and important one. Saul had been imprisoning Christians, but Ananias put his faith in Jesus to protect him and, through his obedience, one of the most important figures in history became a witness to Jesus and established churches throughout the Roman world. Saul received the Holy Spirit and his healing through the laying on of hands. The first Ananias lied to the Holy Spirit and died in Acts 5.

God is sovereign; however, this is the Bible pattern of how he prefers to operate on earth; through the laying on of hands by believers.

Acts 9:17

> And Ananias went his way and entered the house; and laying his hands on him he said, "Brother Saul, the Lord Jesus, who appeared to you on the road as you came, has sent me that you may receive your sight and be filled with the Holy Spirit."

Third, when Saul answered this calling, his nature and purpose in life changed dramatically and his name was changed from Saul to Paul from the time of Acts 13:9.

Paul was traveling on one of his great journeys throughout the Mediterranean region and arrived in the city of Ephesus, which is in modern-day Turkey. He found a group of people who appeared to be believers but had only been introduced to John's baptism. Paul began to teach them, as we saw in the previous chapter.

Acts 19:

> 5 When they heard this, they were baptized in the name of the Lord Jesus.
> 6 When Paul laid hands on them, the Holy Spirit came upon them, and they spoke with tongues and prophesied.

Paul knew that God is sovereign and could impart the Holy Spirit any way He chose, but He preferred to impart the Holy Spirit by the laying on of hands. He had received the Holy Spirit that way and he practiced the same means of impartation himself.

Imparting Spiritual Gifts and Power

Spiritual gifts and anointing can also be passed on to a person through the laying on of hands.

In 1 Timothy 4:14, Paul says:

> Do not neglect the gift that is in you, which was given to you by prophecy with the laying on of the hands of the eldership.

God chooses to operate this way through the body of Christ, using the hands of believers laid on and touching other believers. Spiritual power is passed on, from God, through one believer to another.

Once when Peter wanted to call fire down on some Samaritans who didn't want them in their village, Jesus had to stop that sort of talk quickly:

Luke 9:55

But He turned and rebuked them, and said, "You do not know what manner of spirit you are of."

Still to this day we don't realize "what manner of spirit" we are. If Jesus hadn't stopped Peter, then fire would have fallen from heaven and destroyed the village. We have real spiritual power at our disposal if we use our faith. Great and mighty gifts and blessings can be released in a person's life through us by the laying on of hands. It is extremely unfortunate that many people don't realize the spiritual power and blessings God has made available for them, and live so far below their spiritual potential. However, as we do learn to operate by faith in the things of God, we need to develop this spiritual authority responsibly and with reverence.

Healing

Healing is also ministered or passed on to a person through the laying on of hands. Human touch creates a connection between people; it is a powerful form of communication. However, when human touch is empowered by faith it needs to be used with even more responsibility and care.

In Luke 8, when the woman with the hemorrhage forced her way through the crowd and touched the edge of Jesus' clothes – in a sense the woman laid hands on Jesus to receive – He felt a power surge.

Luke 8:

45 And Jesus said, "who touched Me?" ...
45 ... "Somebody touched Me, for I perceived power going out from Me."

I wonder what the disciples made of His comment with all of those people crowding around and jostling Him. But He felt power go out from Him because someone with faith just managed to touch the hem of His garment. That was all she needed; just a touch of the hem of His clothes and she expected miracle-working power to flow through her body and heal a problem she'd had for twelve years.

Jesus healed people in a number of ways. He spoke the Word and the centurion's servant was healed (Matthew 8:5–13). He made mud with His spit and put it on a blind man's eyes then told him to wash it off to restore his sight (John 9:6). He also laid hands on people.

The first time He visited Nazareth after He began His ministry, He wasn't accepted by the people but He still healed some by laying His hands on them.

Mark 6:

5   Now He could do no mighty work there, except that He laid His hands on a few sick people and healed them.
6   And He marveled because of their unbelief.

Mark 8:

22   Then He came to Bethsaida; and they brought a blind man to Him and begged Him to touch him.
23   So He took the blind man by the hand and led him out of the town. And when He had spit on his eyes and put His hands on him, He asked him if he saw anything.
24   And he looked up and said, "I see men like trees, walking."

25 Then He put His hands on his eyes again and made him look up. And he was restored and saw everyone clearly.

Mark 16:

17 … And these signs will follow those who believe: In My name they will cast out demons; they will speak with new tongues;
18 they will take up serpents; and if they drink anything deadly, it will by no means hurt them; they will lay hands on the sick, and they will recover.

Jesus used this means of healing people and commissioned believers to do the same. The early church was obedient to what Jesus taught about laying on of hands for healing.
Acts 5:12

And through the hands of the apostles many signs and wonders were done among the people.

It doesn't specifically say healing in that particular passage but it is included because this is what happened in Acts 3:7. As soon as Peter touched a lame man and lifted him up he was healed.
When Paul and Barnabas were ministering at Iconium, they laid hands on people to impart a blessing and perform miracles in people's lives.
Acts 14:3

Therefore they stayed there a long time, speaking boldly in the Lord, who was bearing witness to the word of His grace, granting signs and wonders to be done by their hands.

While Paul was ministering in Ephesus, the anointing on him was so strong that people were healed when he laid hands on them, and even if he touched pieces of cloth like handkerchiefs and these were laid on the sick. That is a wonderful empowering by the Holy Spirit that believers are still able to employ in ministering to the sick and that through faith they will recover.

Acts 19:

11   Now God worked unusual miracles by the hands of Paul,
12   so that even handkerchiefs or aprons were brought from his body to the sick, and the diseases left them and the evil spirits went out of them.

Jesus laid hands on people to minister healing. Peter did, and so did Paul and Barnabas. This was the practice of the early church in ministering to the sick. It is a God-ordained means of ministering healing and life to people, and one that we should follow today.

Dedication for Service

There is an example in the Old Testament of laying hands on people to consecrate them for service. When the Levites were dedicated to the Lord, hands were laid on them.

Numbers 8:

10   So you shall bring the Levites before the Lord, and the children of Israel shall lay their hands on the Levites;

> 11 and Aaron shall offer the Levites before the Lord, like a wave offering from the children of Israel, that they may perform the work of the Lord.

This is part of the ceremony whereby the Levites were offered to the Lord so that they could "service the tabernacle of meeting" (Numbers 8:15). They were not allowed to perform any service of ministry until hands were laid on them to offer them to the Lord.

As the early church began to grow, there were administration problems and there was a need to develop other forms of ministry in the church. The twelve apostles decided to appoint seven men to assist with the care of the church and the distribution of food to the widows.

Acts 6:6

> whom they set before the apostles; and when they had prayed, they laid hands on them.

As the church matured and the Holy Spirit wanted to take the gospel throughout the world, He prompted the church in Antioch to come together to pray.

Acts 13:

> 2 As they ministered to the Lord and fasted, the Holy Spirit said, "Now separate to Me Barnabas and Saul for the work to which I have called them."
> 3 Then, having fasted and prayed, and laid hands on them, they sent them away.

This was a commissioning and dedication for service that was imparted through the laying on of hands. The Holy Spirit led the prophets and teachers who were gathered together to send out Barnabas and Saul through the laying on of hands. An anointing was transferred to them by this means. It wasn't a nice but meaningless ceremony; it was the real thing, God's supernatural realm. It was the empowering of the Holy Spirit that saves, heals, delivers and raises the dead to take the Good News to the world.

This was the church that turned the whole world upside down. An anointing from God was imparted to individual believers time after time to break bondages and destroy yokes of oppression by the laying on of hands. This is one of the "elementary principles of Christ" in Hebrews 6:1, which the church taught and was obedient to and still needs today. The laying on of hands is something that God has given the church so that individual believers, as well as the leadership, can be a channel for God's grace and blessings.

VI
Resurrection of the Dead

There is a need for a personal resurrection because when sin came into the world it brought death with it (Romans 5:12). The Greek word for resurrection, *anastasis*, means 'rising up' and 'to cause to stand' (Vines p. 290). All the believers who have died before Jesus returns will have their bodies reconstituted and will rise up out of their graves. Jesus paid for our personal resurrection as part of our redemption.

The Bible talks about three forms of death: physical, spiritual and eternal. It's good to be a believer because we have been redeemed from each of these. The day is coming when we will experience our own resurrection.

Physical Death

We all know that we age and that one day our bodies will die. However, accepting that can be difficult. Changes occur in our bodies to remind us we're mortal. We gradually lose energy, the physical and mental ability to function and we start to become more dependent upon others.

A Spiritual Foundation for Christians

We don't want to be separated from family or friends and everything we have known in this life. Death creates uncertainty to the person with little or no knowledge of God's Word. What is waiting beyond the grave? Where do you go when you die? What do you do? Will you be able to find loved ones and friends?

How people can live this life without believing in life after death is beyond me. To live with that sort of unbelief and uncertainty is too hard, and it is no wonder that anyone who thinks like that will be depressed. As unbelief is increasing in society, so is depression. Those who believe in Jesus have an assurance about the resurrection of the dead and life after death.

A belief in the Biblical teaching of the resurrection of the dead gives great peace and allows a person to get on with life, set free from the anxiety of growing old and dying. An elderly man once said to me that when he became a believer in later life, all the fear was gone. Praise God; that's the only way to live – no fear!

Hebrews 2:

14 Inasmuch then as the children have partaken of flesh and blood, He Himself likewise shared in the same, that through death He might destroy him who had the power of death, that is, the devil,
15 and release those who through fear of death were all their lifetime subject to bondage.

Jesus had to experience death and rise from it to destroy it. It was not God's original intention that we would die. That is a consequence of sin.

Michael McKeon

Romans 5:12

Therefore, just as through one man sin entered the world, and death through sin, and thus death spread to all men, because all sinned –

Adam's sin caused God to initiate plan B – redemption. The original plan for life on earth did not include death. Adam's sin led to his own death, and death spread to all men and women because we've all sinned.

We have to navigate our way through a life that has many risks and pressures as well as opportunities. There are many challenges and milestones for us to overcome and achieve. For many they are looking at the clock and are worried that time is running out. Our human spirit feels the need for a right relationship with God and becomes anxious the closer we get to the moment of death if it doesn't have that relationship. It is always possible to repent and receive forgiveness in this life.

Not all believers have answered the calling they knew was in their life, and this is a regret they feel the closer they get to death as well. However, not only can we repent, but I believe we can also ask Him for a longer life to answer our calling or work on unfinished business.

God doesn't want us to live in fear. One of the purposes of Jesus' life and death was "that through death He might destroy him who had the power of death, that is the devil." (Hebrews 2:14)

When someone dies, people sometimes make the mistake of blaming God. That's not fair. The Bible said that the devil had the power of death. Jesus called him the thief who only visits to steal, kill and destroy (John 10:10). If we believe that Jesus' death destroyed the devil's power over believers, he won't have

A Spiritual Foundation for Christians

the power of death over us. I believe that God is able to protect our lives so that the devil is prevented from taking our lives before it's time for us to go. We don't have to live in fear of death anymore.

John 10:10:

> The thief does not come except to steal, and to kill, and to destroy. I have come that they may have life, and that they may have it more abundantly.

We should spend time with Jesus and believe for more and a better quality of life. Unfortunately, some believers die young or in tragic circumstances. Paul said it well in 1 Corinthians 13:12: "For now we see through a glass darkly..." (King James Version). We don't see everything clearly and we don't understand everything yet. One day these things will be revealed to us.

A pastor's adult son developed cancer and died. The pastor said that many people had received healing from cancer after he had prayed, but his son died. He prayed and asked the Lord about it. The answer he believes he received was that this was the only way the Lord could have saved his son. The pastor didn't mean that God put cancer on him, but that God allowed his son to die with cancer. I also believe that if you have accomplished what God put you here to do, it doesn't really matter when you die or how you die. The main thing is that you were obedient to your calling. God wants us to know many things but we don't know everything in this life. Ultimately, we have to live trusting Him.

God wants to assure us that those who believe in Him will live with Him forever. He is our Father, God. We are His children and He doesn't want to be separated from us any longer than is necessary. He will raise us from the dead and out of the grave to be with Him.

Death is not the end of existence; it's like being born into a new life. Our physical bodies die but they will live again. God is the source of life; He has "life in Himself" (John 5:26). That's amazing. He's the source of it all; He's God all by Himself.

Spiritual Death

Spiritual death is the state of the human spirit that is not saved or in a right relationship with God. The person is spiritually dead to God. Their spirit cannot receive from God in that state and they must be born again during the probation period given to men and women, which is life on earth. Even though their body is physically very much alive, their spirit cannot receive from God in that state.

If a person rejects and doesn't believe Jesus is God, they live in the sin of unbelief. Once a person becomes a believer in Jesus and is born again, it is possible to lose their right relationship with God through sin and fall back into spiritual death.

Romans 6:23

> For the wages of sin is death, but the gift of God is eternal life in Christ Jesus our Lord.

Sin is a problem for anyone who wants to continue in that behavior. God has dealt with the problem by sending Jesus to pay the price for sin and redeem us to Himself. It's not God's desire for anyone to perish. If we sin then repent, we will be forgiven. The whole plan of redemption was to ransom men and women back to God from a state of sin, even at the cost of Jesus' life. Eternal life is a gift. We have a choice; we don't have to be or live as spiritually dead people. We need to choose wisely in life as the consequences are eternal.

Eternal Death

Finally, there is eternal death, also known as the second death, whereby our eternal spirit is condemned to eternal separation from God. This is damnation. It is the ultimate ruin and loss a person can experience, but it is not the end of existence.

John 5:

24   Most assuredly, I say to you, he who hears My word and believes in Him who sent Me has everlasting life, and shall not come into judgment, but has passed from death into life.
25   Most assuredly, I say to you, the hour is coming, and now is, when the dead will hear the voice of the Son of God; and those who hear will live.
26   For as the Father has life in Himself, so He has granted the Son to have life in Himself,
27   and has given Him authority to execute judgment also, because He is the Son of Man.
28   Do not marvel at this; for the hour is coming in which all who are in the graves will hear His voice
29   and come forth – those who have done good, to the resurrection of life, and those who have done evil, to the resurrection of condemnation.

Revelation 20:

6   Blessed and holy is he who has part in the first resurrection. Over such the second death has no power, but they shall be priests of God and of Christ, and shall reign with Him a thousand years.
11 Then I saw a great white throne and Him who sat on it, from whose face the earth and the heaven fled away. And there was found no place for them.
12 And I saw the dead, small and great, standing before God, and books were opened. And another book was opened, which is the Book of Life. And the dead were judged according to their works, by the things which were written in the books.
13 The sea gave up the dead who were in it, and Death and Hades delivered up the dead who were in them. And they were judged, each one according to his works.
14 Then Death and Hades were cast into the lake of fire. This is the second death.
15 And anyone not found written in the Book of Life was cast into the lake of fire.

When Jesus raised Lazarus from the dead, He told Martha that He was "…the resurrection and the life." (John 11:25.) Paul put it this way:
1 Corinthians 15:45

And so it is written, "The first man Adam became a living being." The last Adam became a life-giving spirit.

The very principle of life is within Jesus. When He says, "I am the resurrection and the life," (John 11:25) it echoes the revelation of God's name and nature to Moses, "I AM WHO I AM." (Exodus 3:14) It's enigmatic, it's mysterious. It's beyond the human. Every time Jesus uses that expression, "I am", He was giving the Jews a giant hint who He was and what He was capable of. They didn't always get it. We need to believe that Jesus is the resurrection and the life and we'll rise up out of the grave as He did.

John 11:

23   Jesus said to her, "Your brother will rise again."
24   Martha said to Him, "I know that he will rise again in the resurrection at the last day."
25   Jesus said to her, "I am the resurrection and the life. He who believes in Me, though he may die, he shall live.
26   And whoever lives and believes in Me shall never die. Do you believe this?"

The only way to know that you will avoid the second death is to believe in Jesus and live in a right relationship with Him.

The Two Resurrections

Everyone born on this earth will experience a resurrection. The Bible teaches that there will be two resurrections. The first is the resurrection of the righteous and the second is the resurrection of the unrighteous. The righteous are made right with God through their belief in Jesus. They have been justified because they believe that Jesus is God and He has paid for their sins.

These are the just; they have been justified by God and then act justly in their relationship with God and people.
Acts 24:15

> I have hope in God, which they themselves also accept, that there will be a resurrection of the dead, both of the just and the unjust.

The first resurrection

The first resurrection will be for the righteous only and will occur at the time when Jesus returns to earth. The Father is the only one who knows when this will be (Matthew 24:36). There was a lot of speculation that the year 2000 would be the time when Jesus would return, but scripture says only that the Father knows. When someone says they know the day or the hour when Jesus will reappear, they are wrong and no one should listen to them.

However, I believe we are getting closer to that time and we need to be aware of the signs of the times and their progressive fulfillment. The clock started ticking when Israel became a nation again in 1948, and God is counting down. I believe that Jesus could return in my lifetime and I live as though He will. It's best that we be ready to go at any time, but as for the actual time of His return we don't know when that will be.

Daniel 12:2

> And many of those who sleep in the dust of the earth shall awake, Some to everlasting life, Some to shame and everlasting contempt.

Luke 14:14

... And you will be blessed, because they cannot repay you; for you shall be repaid at the resurrection of the just.

Revelation 20:

4   And I saw thrones, and they sat on them, and judgment was committed to them. Then I saw the souls of those who had been beheaded for their witness to Jesus and for the word of God, who had not worshiped the beast or his image, and had not received his mark on their foreheads or on their hands. And they lived and reigned with Christ for a thousand years.
5   But the rest of the dead did not live again until the thousand years were finished. This is the first resurrection.
6   Blessed and holy is he who has part in the first resurrection. Over such the second death has no power, but they shall be priests of God and of Christ, and shall reign with Him a thousand years.

The Sadducees (Matthew 22:23) believed that there was no resurrection. They must be the sorriest group of people you'll find in the Bible. They were a powerful group of priests who held a more rigid interpretation of the law than the Pharisees. However, for all their pious religiosity, they were the only ones who couldn't find a reference to the resurrection in scripture. There must be a lesson about spiritual blindness to be learned from these people. We mustn't think we know it all. We need to guard our hearts so that we will be humble before God and His Word, so He can reveal His truth to us and make us free.

There are references in the Old Testament to the resurrection. Job believed that after he died he would see his Redeemer in the flesh.

Job 19:

25 For I know that my Redeemer lives, and He shall stand at last on the earth;
26 And after my skin is destroyed, this I know, That in my flesh I shall see God,

David also believed in a personal bodily resurrection.

Psalm 17:15:

As for me, I will see Your face in righteousness; I shall be satisfied when I awake in Your likeness.

Jesus spoke several times about the resurrection, as I have quoted. He taught it, and He died to be "the first born from the dead" (Colossians 1:18).

The early church believed in and taught the resurrection of the dead. Paul taught that there will be a physical resurrection of the body of the righteous. It's worth reading all of chapter 15 of Paul's first letter to the church in Corinth as it discusses death and resurrection.

1 Corinthians 15:

21 For since by man came death, by Man also came the resurrection of the dead.
22 For as in Adam all die, even so in Christ all shall be made alive.

A Spiritual Foundation for Christians

We are born into this world with an earthly body, which is capable and gifted. The human body is a miracle of God's creation. Ecclesiastes, 11:5, asks how bones grow in the womb? We should be in awe of what God has done. However, as complex and beautiful as the earthly body is, the best is yet to come. When Jesus raises us from the dead we will have a glorious body similar to His. It will look like us but perfect and enhanced, without a single imperfection. We will recognize those we have known on earth but we will all have a glorified body.

1 Corinthians 15:

49 And as we have borne the image of the man of dust, we shall also bear the image of the heavenly Man.
50 Now this I say, brethren, that flesh and blood cannot inherit the kingdom of God; nor does corruption inherit incorruption.
51 Behold, I tell you a mystery; We shall not all sleep, but we shall all be changed –
52 in a moment, in the twinkling of an eye, at the last trumpet. For the trumpet will sound, and the dead will be raised incorruptible, and we shall be changed.

Our glorified bodies will "bear the image of the heavenly man" (verse 49). Our bodies will have the same qualities that Jesus' body had when He rose from the dead. His body appeared to share supernatural and natural qualities. Jesus could suddenly appear amongst the disciples, as if into locked rooms, and eat food in front of them, proving that he wasn't a disembodied spirit. He could be touched and recognized by those who knew Him (Luke 24:36–43). We will share His image and state and be able to do likewise.

These new bodies will live in "incorruption" (verse 50). They will not age or be afflicted by illness to experience death again. Without the resurrection there would be nothing to look forward to. That body that reached its peak in youth would only ever deteriorate after that point. Fortunately, there is the promise of a permanently glorious body.

We are a spirit, we have a soul (a mind, will and emotions), and we live in a body. Life and resurrection isn't just about our bodies raising up out of the ground as a glorified body. Our spirits will live forever with God in those heavenly bodies. While on earth, our spirit needed an earth suit. When we get to heaven, we will need a body fit for purpose, to dwell in the presence and glory of God.

When Paul wrote to the Thessalonians about the resurrection, he was led to say that he didn't want the church to be ignorant. God wants us to know what's going to happen. He doesn't want us to sorrow and grieve like the world that doesn't know His Word. I like the way God told Moses he was going to die in Deuteronomy 32:50. God told Moses that he would "be gathered to his people", just like Aaron was. Death brings a separation from those left alive on earth, but it also brings a reunion with those believers who have gone before.

Those believers who have already died will be the first to rise up out of their graves, wherever they are, and meet the Lord. Then, those believers who are alive at the time of Jesus' return will rise up from earth and join Jesus and the other believers in the atmosphere. God doesn't want us to be ignorant or afraid, He wants us to be assured and prepared for that day.

A Spiritual Foundation for Christians

1 Thessalonians 4:

13 But I do not want you to be ignorant, brethren, concerning those who have fallen asleep, lest you sorrow as others who have no hope.
14 For if we believe that Jesus died and rose again, even so God will bring with Him those who sleep in Jesus.
15 For this we say to you by the word of the Lord, that we who are alive and remain until the coming of the Lord will by no means precede those who are asleep.
16 For the Lord Himself will descend from heaven with a shout, with the voice of an archangel, and with the trumpet of God. And the dead in Christ will rise first.
17 Then we who are alive and remain shall be caught up together with them in the clouds to meet the Lord in the air. And thus we shall always be with the Lord.

He wants us to be expecting His return, going about our Father's business. We need to be like the "good and faithful servants" from the parable of the talents in Matthew 25:14–30: "After a long time", verse 19, Jesus is returning to the earth. We need to be eagerly waiting for Him as the writer of Hebrews encourages us (Hebrews 9:28), and not caught acting as though He's never coming back.

The second resurrection

The bad news (for some) is that there will be a resurrection for the unrighteous. This is a separate resurrection that will take place 1,000 years after the first. Revelation chapter 20, verses 5 to 6 and 12 to 15, speak of this.

Revelation 20:

5   But the rest of the dead did not live again until the thousand years were finished. This is the first resurrection.
6   Blessed and holy is he who has part in the first resurrection. Over such the second death has no power, but they shall be priests of God and of Christ, and shall reign with Him a thousand years.
12   And I saw the dead, small and great, standing before God, and books were opened. ... And the dead were judged according to their works, by the things which were written in the books.
13   And the sea gave up the dead who were in it, and Death and Hades delivered up the dead who were in them ...
14   Then Death and Hades were cast into the lake of fire. This is the second death.
15   And anyone not found written in the Book of Life was cast into the lake of fire.

John 5:29:

28   Do not marvel at this; for the hour is coming in which all who are in the graves will hear His voice
29   and come forth – those who have done good, to the resurrection of life, and those who have done evil, to the resurrection of condemnation.

Daniel 12:2:

> And many of those who sleep in the dust of the earth shall awake, Some to everlasting life, Some to shame and everlasting contempt.

The 1,000-year reign of Jesus and all those who take part in the first resurrection is an amazing phenomenon. Scripture doesn't say much about it but I think that we will experience life on earth the way God originally intended it. We will "be priests of God and of Christ, and shall reign with Him a thousand years." There's no more sacrifice for sin but we will be able to offer our praise to God. Revelation 20:6 promises we will rule and reign with Jesus for the 1000 years.

Belief and obedience determines where a person spends eternity. Those who have believed in the God of the Bible and obeyed Him will have a part in the first resurrection. Sadly, not everyone will. There are those who say they don't believe a loving God could send people to hell. They need to read the Bible and see what God says Himself. There is a separation between those who choose faithfulness and obedience to God and those who rebel against Him. Jesus said that Himself numerous times: the parable of the wedding feast (Matthew 22:1–14); the parable of the wise and foolish virgins (Matthew 25:1–13); the parable of the talents (Matthew 25:14–30); and the son of man will judge the nations (Matthew 25:31–46). He doesn't want people to be separated from Him but he has given us a choice.

God will not tolerate sin. Jesus died to pay the price for our sin and we need to believe that in this life.

Those who are a part of the second resurrection will experience eternal "shame and everlasting contempt" (Daniel 12:2). "Everlasting" is a long time. Usually, we can endure something when we know that it is for a short time, but everlasting shame and contempt should be avoided if we have any sense at all. However, it is what that person deserves if they don't repent and turn toward God and away from sinful behavior. If a person refuses to worship God and obey His commandments, then that person must be incarcerated for the protection of those who do. God has standards that are just.

VII

Eternal Judgment

There is One God and There is a Judgment

We are already going to live forever, somewhere, in some state. Eternity is a long time and we should carefully consider our options. The sad fact is that our bodies physically deteriorate and, on a day already known to God, we'll die. Our bodies will return to the basic elements of the earth because the real us, our spirit, has departed. "…for dust you are, and to dust you shall return." (Genesis 3:19)

It is futile to deny that there is a judgment that will determine how we spend eternity. Societies and cultures all around the world experience the supernatural. They don't just believe in the supernatural, they experience it and they believe in some form of judgment and life after death.

Scientists vary in their opinion on whether there is a creator or not. Science can only know what it can observe and measure, but God is a Spirit (John 4:24), and He created everything that is observed and measured. Science certainly knows some things, but it doesn't know everything. Those scientists who don't believe that there is a God have to explain the initial creation of matter and the laws that govern the universe. I don't know all the details of how God created the universe but I know that He did.

Genesis 1:1

> In the beginning God created the heavens and the earth.

There's no such thing as mother nature as a creative force; there's only God's nature. God endowed life on earth with the ability to reproduce itself with encoded DNA "whose seed is within itself" (Genesis 1:11). The principle of genetics, the reproduction of life, yet incorporating the capacity for individuality, gives us insight into the nature of God.

Genesis 1:11

> Then God said, "Let the earth bring forth grass, the herb that yields seed, and the fruit tree that yields fruit according to its kind, whose seed is in itself, on the earth"; and it was so.

Billions of tons of water move across the surface of the earth from one side of the ocean to the other without disturbing the rotation of the earth by a second. Night follows day in perfect timing every day, every year. God has measured the seas; He knows their depth, volume and their weight. He has measured space. He has weighed the mountains and the hills to give the earth stability.

A Spiritual Foundation for Christians

Isaiah 40:12:

Who has measured the waters in the hollow of His hand,
Measured heaven with a span
And calculated the dust of the earth in a measure?
Weighed the mountains in scales
And the hills in a balance?

It is amazing and God did it. He keeps creation in perfect balance. To say there is no God takes a denial of the evidence of creation. I think atheism is magical realism; you have to imagine something else besides the evidence. I believe a person should live prepared to meet their maker. Don't leave it to the last minute; know that God wants to be in a relationship with you and obey Him.

There are many churches that don't satisfy the searching heart. Keep asking, searching and knocking and you will be satisfied (Matthew 7:8). Don't let your search for the deeper things of God be brought to a stop by the dead end of tradition. Don't give up on God because of the actions of some Christians and ministers who should know better but may have offended you.

We have to give account of our lives to God, not to a church or to a man but to God. We would be wise to please God while we are here on earth. This time on earth is a probation period. God is watching to see what type of person we choose to become during our lives and whether we can be trusted with responsibility in this life and the next.

We will be doing something in the millennium reign of Jesus and for all eternity. In the parable of the minas (Luke 19:11–27), those "good servants" who were responsible with minas or finances were rewarded with responsibility over cities for their obedience and diligence.

In the parable of the talents (Matthew 25:14–30), the "good and faithful" servants were told they would be made "ruler over many things. Enter into the joy of your lord." (Verse 23) There will be purposeful activity in the next life and the good and faithful servants in this life will be given more responsibility and the joy of the Lord in the next.

The Bible tells us that there will be a judgment. Jesus tells us there will be a judgment. I'm not perfect but I'm forgiven and I am going to do whatever it takes to hear Jesus say, "Well done good and faithful servant... Enter into the Joy of the Lord," Matthew 25:21.

The Greek word for judgment is *krisis* (Strong's #2920). It means decision for or against, and it implies justice. When used specifically under the jurisdiction of divine law, it means accusation, condemnation and damnation.

It appears that the English word *crisis* originated from the Greek word for judgment and damnation. Damnation certainly is a crisis. This life on earth is a time of probation; we are on trial. Once we die there is no going back, there are no more chances.

There will be a judgment and a separation of people. This truth is repeated throughout scripture. Perhaps this is one of the things that people fear about dying, that there really will be a judgment and everything about them will be exposed to a righteous and just judgment.

Jesus is the Judge

Jesus will be that judge. Here are three scriptures that settle that question.

John 5:22

> For the Father judges no one, but has committed all judgment to the Son,

Romans 2:16

> in the day when God will judge the secrets of men by Jesus Christ, according to my gospel.

2 Corinthians 5:10

> For we must all appear before the judgment seat of Christ, that each one may receive the things done in the body, according to what he has done, whether good or bad.

It is important that we are aware that what we do here on earth has eternal consequences. We are accountable to Jesus for the conduct of our lives, whether we believe in Him or not. We will come before His judgment seat and receive our reward or our punishment according to our own choices.

There are those who blaspheme Jesus. They say He is not God and didn't rise from the dead. They are making a mistake. It is better to live in reverence and obedience before our judge and our King rather than come before Him in fear of the consequences of our rebellion.

The Saints Will Share Governance with Jesus

The saints or believers will not judge other believers, but will share a future role of judgment and administration with Jesus over the world and the angels. 1 Corinthians 6:2–3 is an interesting passage. Paul is admonishing the believers in the Corinthian church, who are disputing with one another in pagan courts when they will have a responsibility for governance themselves.

Believers need to see themselves the way God does. We will be ruling and reigning with the Anointed. We shouldn't be in a hurry to go to court against other believers. Bible-believing Christians should be able to come to an agreement over the matters that concern them without having to have their differences settled by a member of the judiciary, who may not be a believer.

1 Corinthians 6:

2 Do you not know that the saints will judge the world? And if the world will be judged by you, are you unworthy to judge the smallest matters?
3 Do you not know that we shall judge angels? How much more, things that pertain to this life?

The Two Judgments

There are two judgments. First, there is the judgment of the righteous, which is a judgment rewarding the believers for whatever they have worked to achieve for the kingdom of God. Second, there is a judgment of the unrighteous, which is a judgment of punishment on unbelief and sin. Payday comes for everyone.

There are also those who haven't had the opportunity to hear the gospel but have lived according to their conscience, and have kept 'the law' without having it in written form. I believe that the grace and justice of God will take that into account.

Romans 2:

14   ... for when Gentiles, who do not have the law, by nature do the things in the law, these, although not having the law, are a law to themselves,
15   who show the work of the law written in their hearts, their conscience also bearing witness, and between themselves their thoughts accusing or else excusing them)
16   in the day when God will judge the secrets of men by Jesus Christ, according to my gospel.

Everyone will give an account of themselves to Jesus. For believers this is not a judgment of whether we are saved – that was settled when we believed in Jesus and that He gave His life and shed His blood for our sin. We will stand before Him without fear and receive the reward for our faith and our service. We all have a calling in our lives, which we need to seek out and fulfill to the best of our abilities. When God sees that we sought to obey Him in the light that we had, He will reward that.

It's good to worship God and obey Him. God rewards those who are His own. Being a Christian is not all one sided, with the believer having to do a lot for God and getting little or nothing in return. There are rewards for obedience. We are made to wear a crown and receive a reward. God has different crowns and rewards for different purposes.

Revelation 22:12

And behold, I am coming quickly, and My reward is with Me, to give to every one according to his work.

The following scripture illustrates these rewards:

- Inheriting the kingdom, Matthew 25:34.
- The imperishable crown, 1 Corinthians 9:25.
- The crown of rejoicing, 1 Thessalonians 2:19.
- The crown of righteousness, 2 Timothy 4:8.
- The crown of life, James 1:12.
- Crowns of Gold, Revelation 4:4.
- The reward for God servants, the prophets and the saints, Revelation 11:18.

The Bible promises us that we will reap what we sow (Galatians 6:7) and that is what tends to happen in life. However, there are some who don't always receive the recognition or the reward they deserve, while others seem to get away with something they should be punished for. Sometimes life just doesn't seem fair.

It may be that we don't receive all of our reward in this life, and those who rebel against God and act unjustly don't receive all of their punishment in this life either. God is just and His justice demands judgment. That judgment carries over into the next life either as reward or punishment. There is judgment on the unrighteous, of that we can be sure. God keeps a book, and full and comprehensive judgment comes to the unrighteous at the great white throne judgment.

The Great White Throne Judgment

The great white throne judgment occurs after the 1,000-year reign of the Jesus at the second resurrection. The great white throne judgment is only for the unrighteous and it is what the

Bible calls the second death. The first death was the physical death of the person's body, the second death is the person's condemnation to hell and eternal separation from God.

Revelation 2:11

> He who has an ear, let him hear what the Spirit says to the churches. He who overcomes shall not be hurt by the second death.

Revelation 20:

> 10 The devil, who deceived them, was cast into the lake of fire and brimstone where the beast and the false prophet are. And they will be tormented day and night forever and ever.
> 11 Then I saw a great white throne and Him who sat on it, from whose face the earth and the heaven fled away. And there was found no place for them.
> 12 And I saw the dead, small and great, standing before God, and books were opened. And another book was opened, which is the Book of Life. And the dead were judged according to their works, by the things written in the books.
> 13 The sea gave up the dead who were in it, and Death and Hades delivered up the dead who were in them. And they were judged, each one according to his works.
> 14 Then Death and Hades were cast into the lake of fire. This is the second death.
> 15 And anyone not found written in the Book of Life was cast into the lake of fire.

Michael McKeon

The Punishment of Hell

In Mark's Gospel, chapter nine, Jesus quotes the last verse of the book of Isaiah, chapter 66 verse 24, where Isaiah warned about the punishment for sin. Jesus said it was better to suffer a disability in this life through the loss of a hand or a foot, or even an eye, if that prevented you from sinning, rather than go to hell for ever (Mark 9:42–48). Jesus certainly believed and taught that there was a hell and that it was a punishment for sin. In the following passage in Mark 9, Jesus quoted Isaiah 66:24 and repeated this warning about the punishment of hell three times to emphasize the seriousness of it.

Mark 9:44:

> where 'Their worm does not die, And the fire is not quenched.'

Mark writes that Jesus quoted the same passage in Isaiah two more times in the same chapter verses 46 and 48 to emphasize the reality of the punishment of hell.

To say there is no hell is unscriptural. Ministers have a very clear responsibility to tell people that the punishment of hell is real and that sin and unbelief have eternal consequences. The prospect of something like remorse and guilt eating away at you for all eternity is too much, let alone anything else. Any sane and rational person will make the decision to do whatever it takes to be right with God, go to heaven and stay out of hell.

The Bible tells us that there are three levels of hell. We tend to use the word hell in a general sense and think it is all one place or state. However, the scriptures give a more detailed understanding of the place where the sentence of eternal judgment is served. There are separate levels within hell for different kinds of offenders, just as there are in an earthly prison. After the great white throne judgment, all three levels of hell will be contained within the final hell: *gehenna*.

The first level of hell

The first level of hell is *sheol*. This is the Hebrew word for the world of the dead (Strong's #7585). The word sheol is also translated in the King James version of the Old Testament as the grave or the pit.

In the Old Testament, all the dead, the righteous and the unrighteous went to sheol. Jesus gives a revealing illustration of sheol in the story of the rich man and Lazarus (Luke 16:19–31). Sheol is described as being divided into two parts. The unrighteous rich man can see his neighbor, Lazarus, with Abraham, but there is "a great gulf fixed" (verse 26); a division between the two regions and no one can pass from one side to the other.

The region set aside for the righteous in sheol was a waiting place of comfort and contentment. Lazarus was seen in "Abraham's bosom" (verse 23). The bosom is the middle of the chest and that's a good place to be. It gives a picture of belonging and contentedness. There is a security there. This is where the righteous dead waited for the death and resurrection of Jesus when the full price for their sin could be paid.

However, the region of the unrighteous in sheol is a place where there is flame and torment.

Luke 16:24

> "Then he cried and said, 'Father Abraham, have mercy on me, and send Lazarus that he may dip the tip of his

finger in water and cool my tongue; for I am tormented in this flame.'

The unrighteous remain in hades until the second resurrection, when they are released for the great white throne judgment. They have proven who they are and what they are capable of. Now they will be judged and the place and state they will spend eternity in will be fixed.

The Hebrew word sheol is translated in Greek as *hades* in the gospels (Strong's #86), meaning the place or state of departed souls, or even the grave. These two words mean the same place. It is where both the righteous and unrighteous dead from the Old Covenant waited.

The second level of hell

The second level of hell is the place of captivity and is reserved for angels who have sinned. This is the Greek word *tartaroo* (sometimes *tartaros*). It is also translated as *hell* (Strong's #5020), and it means to incarcerate in eternal torment in the deepest abyss of hades. Tartaroo is the place and the state where those angels who rebelled against God in prehistory were restrained. I believe that these unrighteous angels who served Satan are the demons that we know from the Bible. Those demons have some freedom to serve their master Satan at present, but during the 1,000-year reign they will be chained and restricted until their judgment.

2 Peter 2:4

> For if God did not spare the angels who sinned, but cast them down to hell and delivered them into chains of darkness, to be reserved for judgment;

Jude

6   And the angels who did not keep their proper domain, but left their own abode, He has reserved in everlasting chains under darkness for the judgment of the great day;

The third level of hell

The third level of hell is the bottomless pit. Some translations also call this the abyss, or the deep. This is where Satan is held captive for the 1,000-year reign of the Anointed and His Anointed (the believers). This indicates that the 1,000-year reign will be free from the struggle with Satan and his demons.
Revelation 20:

1   Then I saw an angel coming down from heaven, having the key to the bottomless pit and a great chain in his hand.
2   He laid hold of the dragon, that serpent of old, who is the Devil and Satan, and bound him for a thousand years;
3   and he cast him into the bottomless pit, and shut him up, and set a seal on him, so that he should deceive the nations no more till the thousand years were finished. But after these things he must be released for a little while.

The New Testament also translates hell as *gehenna* (Strong's #1067). Literally, this is the valley of (the son of) Hinnom and is a form of ge-hinnom; a valley near Jerusalem. Figuratively, it means everlasting punishment; hell. This is the meaning of hell that we are generally familiar with; the hell of damnation where there is no hope of release. Jesus used the word eleven times in the gospels. All the levels of hell are contained within gehenna and that includes "the lake of fire" (Revelation 20:10–15).

In the actual valley of Hinnom there was a place called tophet, which means altar. This was a place of worship for a manifestation of Satan called Molech. The people worshiped Molech here centuries before by sacrificing their children in fire (Jerimiah 7:31–32). In Jesus' time the area was used as a rubbish dump for Jerusalem. There was everything associated with such a place; the carcasses of dead animals, rotting food, foul smells and flies. The place was continually burning, consuming what was defiled. This was the image Jesus wanted to communicate when He used the word gehenna.

Luke 12:5:

But I will show you whom you should fear; Fear Him who, after He has killed, has power to cast into hell; yes I say to you, fear Him!

Satan is God's creation and He is going to take responsibility for dealing with that troublemaker. Satan will not escape judgment and punishment for all the evil and all the pain he has caused. He will be called to his creator to give account for every single action. He will reap back all the trouble, every heartache, every sickness and all the fear he has sown into the lives of humankind. It is worth repeating his future.

Revelation 20:10:

The devil, who deceived them, was cast into the lake of fire and brimstone where the beast and the false prophet are. And they will be tormented day and night forever and ever.

In summary those who have died and are not in a right relationship with God will wait in the region of sheol where there is flame and torment for the great white throne judgement. Jesus used the word gehenna for hell in the gospels. All the levels of hell are included within gehenna. At the white throne judgement people are condemned to hell.

The Redeemed in Paradise

Once Jesus arose from the dead, the region of sheol/hades for the redeemed has always been spoken of as being up rather than down. Paul was taken up to paradise.

2 Corinthians 12:
3 And I know such a man – whether in the body or out of the body I do not know, God knows –
4 how he was caught up into Paradise...

Prior to this, all mention of sheol/hades was located down, inside the earth.
Ephesians 4:

8 Therefore He says;
"When He ascended on high,
He led captivity captive,
And gave gifts to men."
9 (Now this, "He ascended" – what does it mean but that He also first descended into the lower parts of the earth?

10 He who descended is also the One who ascended far above all the heavens, that He might fill all things.)

This passage from Ephesians 4 tells us something of what happened between Jesus' death and when He had ascended to His Father in heaven. Peter reflects the same teaching as Paul saying that after Jesus died, "...He went and preached to the spirits in prison" (1 Peter 3:19).

Jesus led "captivity captive" (verse 8). He paraded His defeated prisoner, Satan, the accuser of the brethren in the sight of heaven and hell. Jesus demonstrated His victory over death and the devil (Hebrews 2:14). This marked a turning point for Satan. Redemption was paid for and Satan's ultimate failure and incarceration were guaranteed.

Paul tells us that Jesus also "descended into the lower parts of the earth" (Ephesians 4:9). Now, this tells us that before Jesus' death, sheol/hades was inside the earth, possibly at or near the center of the earth. Then, after the atoning work of Jesus on the cross, the righteous dead were released into the presence of God.

Jesus promised the repentant criminal on the cross that: "Assuredly, I say to you, today you will be with Me in Paradise." (Luke 23:43) Paradise was originally a Persian word for garden, however, it came to be a term for the dwelling place of the righteous. I believe that this is the best way to understand Paradise because the dwelling place of the righteous moved. Therefore, the repentant criminal was with Jesus in sheol on the day they died and later entered the presence of God the Father.

It appears from scripture that Jesus didn't enter the presence of the Father between his death and resurrection; this occurred later. Therefore, if Jesus did not enter the presence of the Father until after the resurrection, it is likely that the righteous entered at the same time or shortly after.

Jesus said to Mary Magdalene on the day of His resurrection, in John 20:17;

> Do not cling to Me, for I have not yet ascended to My Father...

His ascension into heaven occurred after His rising from the dead, even after He had spoken to Mary Magdalene, but apparently before He appeared amongst the disciples, since He asked Thomas to put his finger into the holes in His hand and his hand into His side (John 20:27).

As can be seen from Revelation 2:7, Paradise is the dwelling place of the redeemed and it is blessed with the eternal life that comes from God.

Revelation 2:7:

> ... To Him who overcomes I will give to eat from the tree of life, which is in the midst of the Paradise of God.

Jesus has moved the part of sheol/hades where the righteous dead were waiting to the immediate presence of God. They are released from waiting to be in the presence of God and their dwelling place is now "in the midst of the Paradise of God". Paradise has moved from the center of the earth to the throne room of God.

Paul said he was confident that to be absent from the body was to be present with the Lord (2 Corinthians 5:8). Jesus isn't in a part of sheol or hades separated from the immediate presence of God, He is "sitting at the right hand of God" (Colossians 3:1). If the righteous dead are with the Lord, and He is sitting at the right hand of the Father, then they must also be in the presence of the Father.

The unrighteous remain in their region of sheol/hades until the second resurrection, when they are released for the great white throne judgment.

The Three Heavens

The Bible speaks about three heavens. The Hebrew word for heaven, *shameh* (Strong's #8064), means to be lofty or higher. Just as the sky is physically higher than the earth, so heaven is spiritually higher than this earth. The Greek word for heaven, *ouranos* (Strong's #3772), means elevation first physically with the sky, and then spiritually, the home of God, and implies happiness, power and eternity.

The first heaven

The first heaven is the atmosphere or sky. It is the heaven where weather patterns are formed and where Satan causes natural disasters. He has the power to cause destructive storms, floods and heart-breaking droughts because this power was given to him as a consequence of Adam's rebellion against God (Luke 4:6). This heaven is likened to the Outer Court of the tabernacle of Moses and temple of Solomon.

The second heaven

The second heaven is the planetary or celestial heaven. It is likened to the Holy Place in the tabernacle of Moses and Solomon. It is the heaven that God spoke to Abram about:

A Spiritual Foundation for Christians

Genesis 15:5:

... Look now toward heaven, and count the stars if you are able to number them."

It is the heaven of untold galaxies that we strive to learn about and explore. It is the universe held in place by God Himself. This heaven, as magnificent as it is to behold, will be shaken.
Isaiah 13:13:

Therefore I will shake the heavens,
and the earth will move out of her place,

Isaiah 34:4:

All the host of heaven shall be dissolved,
And the heavens shall be rolled up like a scroll;
All their host shall fall down
As the leaf falls from the vine,
And as fruit falling from a fig tree.

Joel 2:10:

The earth quakes before them,
The heavens tremble;
The sun and moon grow dark,
And the stars diminish their brightness.

The earth will be shaken on its orbit. The existing heaven and earth will be rolled up like a scroll and dissolve. Our solar system and the galaxies will no longer maintain their positions and there will be great chaos in the universe. Then God will create a new heaven and a new earth, which He has been waiting to put in place (Revelation 21:1). This earth is going to pass away with everything on it. We need to have a Bible perspective to life. Many times, people strive for things that will not last. It's best to have our priorities right and invest in treasure that will last forever, rather than something that will not stand the test of time.

There are sometimes accounts of unidentified flying objects, and science searches for evidence of other forms of life. In a natural human or scientific sense this is amazing, but from a spiritual point of view it really doesn't matter whether there is other intelligent life or not. If there is life on other planets, then God created it, and if this life has an eternal spirit, then Jesus is their redeemer also.

The third heaven

The third heaven is the dwelling place of God. It's true that God the Father is for us, Jesus is with us and we can be filled with the Holy Spirit, but God's throne is in the third heaven. The dwelling place of God in the throne room is the model for the Holy of Holies in Moses' tabernacle and Solomon's temple.

Paul was given a revelation of the third heaven. He didn't really know whether he was in his body at the time or not but he knew that he had been taken up to the third heaven to the presence of God Himself. Paul says, in 2 Corinthians 12:4, that he heard words that he could not repeat. Paul doesn't tell us what he saw, only that he heard "words" of a quality and a dimension that we haven't experienced. We don't know if they were statements or dialog, who they were spoken by or between, but this communication was too sacred and perhaps not able to be spoken in the limited vocabulary of human language.

2 Corinthians 12:

2   I know a man in Christ who fourteen years ago – whether in the body I do not know, or whether out of the body I do not know, God knows – such a one was caught up to the third heaven.
3   And I know such a man – whether in the body or out of the body I do not know, God knows –
4   how he was caught up into Paradise and heard inexpressible words, which it is not lawful for a man to utter.

When John wrote his revelation, he said he was "in the Spirit on the Lord's day" (Revelation 1:10). John has given us a description of the third heaven. The reason John was shown the throne room and that he also heard what was said was so that he could be witness to it. This was a different revelation with a different purpose. These words must be communicated.

Revelation 4:

2   Immediately I was in the Spirit; and behold, a throne set in heaven and One sat on the throne.
1   And He who sat there was like a jasper and a sardius stone in appearance; and there was a rainbow around the throne, in appearance like an emerald.

The "One" God sitting on the throne is described in terms of symbolic qualities rather than specific features. Jasper is most likely a diamond, pure in quality and brilliant in glory. A sardius stone is a deep red. The blood of God has been shed by Jesus' atoning death for sin and the time is at hand for God's great anger to be poured out on sin that has not been repented of. The sardius and the jasper are the first and the last of the twelve precious stones on the High Priest's breastplate. The emerald was also one of the twelve stones (Exodus 28:17–21).

There is a rainbow around the throne of emerald appearance. Emerald green is a color that rests the eyes and symbolizes mercy. The rainbow was the sign of God's covenant to Noah (Genesis 9:15–17). God's covenant relationship with His children is everlasting and is made from a desire to be merciful.

There are those alive today who say they have visited heaven. I believe a number of these accounts. As the time comes closer for Jesus to return, I believe the church will experience more and more of God's sovereign revelation of His Love and His Glory and more of His people will be allowed profound experiences and revelations.

The New Heaven and the New Earth

Revelation 21:

1. Now I saw a new heaven and a new earth, for the first heaven and the first earth had passed away. Also there was no more sea.
2. Then I, John, saw the holy city, New Jerusalem, coming down out of heaven from God, prepared as a bride adorned for her husband.
3. And I heard a loud voice from heaven saying, "Behold, the tabernacle of God is with men, and He will dwell with them, and they shall be His

people. God Himself will be with them and be their God.

4   And God will wipe away every tear from their eyes; there shall be no more death, nor sorrow, nor crying. There shall be no more pain, for the former things have passed away."

5   Then He who sat on the throne said, "Behold, I make all things new." And He said to me, "Write, for these words are true and faithful."

6   And He said to me, "It is done! I am the Alpha and the Omega, the Beginning and the End. I will give of the fountain of the water of life freely to him who thirsts.

7   He who overcomes shall inherit all things, and I will be his God and he shall be My son.

8   But the cowardly, unbelieving, abominable, murderers, sexually immoral, sorcerers, idolaters, and all liars shall have their part in the lake which burns with fire and brimstone, which is the second death."

11 … having the glory of God. Her light was like a most precious stone, like a jasper stone, clear as crystal.

22 But I saw no temple in it, for the Lord God Almighty and the Lamb are its temple.

27 But there shall by no means enter it anything that defiles, or causes an abomination or a lie, but only those who are written in the Lamb's Book of Life.

Revelation 21, verse 1, tells us that the current heaven and earth will not last forever but will be replaced. There will be great changes to the new earth. There will be no more sea. This is a symbol of separation between people and the place of storms and danger. The beast comes out of the sea (Revelation 13:1) and these things will no longer afflict humankind.

Verse 2: Jerusalem will be recreated not just changed. It will come down out of heaven to take its place and fulfill its purpose. It will be a holy city, not one that has been compromised by sin, the death of prophets and God's only begotten son. Jerusalem herself is "prepared as a bride adorned for her husband" (Revelation 21:2). This description is the covenant language of marriage. It speaks of the deeply personal relationship between two covenant partners. Jerusalem is prepared in the same loving way as a bride prepares herself for her husband on their wedding day. This reflects the everlasting covenant relationship between God and His people.

Verse 3: God's tabernacle or dwelling place is no longer separate from His people but is now amongst them. Just as Jesus was Immanuel – God with us on earth – so the redeemed will dwell with God the Father, Son and Holy Spirit in the new heaven. We will not only know God by faith, but we will see His face and live in His presence. That spiritual hunger will be satisfied as God is no longer "hidden" but He dwells with the redeemed and will manifest Himself in the fullness of His glory.

Verse 4: In the endless life in the new heaven there will be no more tears to cry, pain to bear or death to grieve. All that is associated with heartache and suffering has passed away with the first heaven and earth. This is the presence of the God who is Love.

Verse 5: God "…calls those things which do not exist as though they did;" (Romans 4:17). Just as God used words to create the first earth and, presumably, the first heaven (Genesis 1:1–24), He will use words to create the new heaven and the new earth. When He says, "Behold, I make all things new", the new heaven and the new earth are called into existence. Words were designed by God to carry meaning and power and God's Word carries infinite power.

Verse 6: God is the first and the last as Alpha and Omega are the first and the last letters of the Greek alphabet. He is the first cause and the perfecter of all creation, including men and women. He is in control. At the time John received this revelation, he had been banished to the Island of Patmos, and the church was under persecution and needed encouragement from God. The church still suffers persecution and there are still martyrs in the world today, but God will take control and make all things new. He will punish the unrighteous and reward those who thirst for righteousness. There is an everlasting source of the "water of life" that God will give "freely". There will be perfect and permanent fulfillment and satisfaction in the new heaven.

Verse 7: Not all people overcome the challenges and temptations of this life, but those who do "shall inherit all things". They shall live in a state without lack or shortage of any good thing. They shall receive an inheritance from God, "who is able to do exceedingly abundantly above all that we ask or think…" (Ephesians 3:20). Those who overcome will enter into the manifested relationship of a son or daughter with their Father, the creator of heaven and earth.

Verse 8: It's not always popular, even among believers, to call out sin, but God will. He has standards of right behavior and it doesn't matter whether community standards change. It is the standard God sets in His Word that will determine whether we are able to enter His presence or be sent from His presence for eternity.

Verse 11: The city is filled with the glory of God. Verses 9–21 describe the New Jerusalem, first as "the bride, the Lamb's wife" (verse 9). Again, this is the language of the covenant relationship between God and His people. The glory of God in the holy city is expressed in terms of precious stones, walls of jasper (diamond) and the city made of pure gold. This is the dwelling place of the God of creation and nothing is impossible to Him. The wealth of the city is extreme by human standards, but this is the city of God.

Verse 22: We will worship, reverence and enjoy the presence of God the Father, God the son, Jesus, and God the Holy Spirit, and will not be restricted to any earthly building. We will live in a state where we cannot sin and will dwell in the presence of love continually, forevermore.

Verse 27: God is a holy God and He will not tolerate the defilement of sin in His kingdom. He was patient and endured it on the old earth until judgment. Now, all those who live in sin, including those described in verse 8, will not be allowed entrance.

Revelation chapter 22 continues this revelation of the glory of the new heaven and the true home of the redeemed. This is where the redeemed belong and this is where they are fully recompensed.

Revelation 22:

1. And he showed me a pure river of water of life, clear as crystal, proceeding from the throne of God and of the Lamb.
2. in the middle of the street, and on either side of the river, was the tree of life which bore twelve fruits, each tree yielding its fruit every month. The leaves of the tree were for the healing of the nations.

Verse 1: The river of life, the source of life itself, flows from the throne and presence of God. The Holy Spirit will flow freely. The Holy Spirit proceeds directly from the presence of God the Father and Jesus. He will be freely available to God's people all the time.

The river is a recurring theme that is used throughout scripture to express abundant spiritual life. Just as a river on this earth brings life everywhere it flows, this "pure river of water of life" brings the life of God to everyone it touches. A river flowed in Eden to water the garden (Genesis 2:10). Zechariah was shown that on the day of the Lord, "living waters shall flow from Jerusalem" (Zechariah 14:8). Ezekiel was given a wonderful revelation of the river. He saw water flowing from under the temple. As it flowed it became deeper and deeper so that it could not be crossed. Everywhere the river flowed it gave life and healing (Ezekiel 47:1–12).

Verse 2: The tree of life is another recurring theme in God's Word. The tree of life was in the garden of Eden (Genesis 3:22–24). Adam and Eve were expelled from the garden in case they were to eat from this tree and live forever in rebellion against God. This is the tree of eternal life and its full significance will be revealed when we reach heaven.

There are also "all kinds of trees" in Ezekiel 47:12; they grow along the bank of the river. They provide abundant fruit and their leaves are used to make people thoroughly whole. There is nothing missing and nothing broken in the New Jerusalem.

The position of this tree is simultaneously "In the middle of its street, and on either side of the river". This is significant and mysterious to us at this time, until its meaning is revealed to us by God. Both the tree and the river are "of life". These two life forces come from God and work together. The works of God complement each other, just as His people should complement each other in their work with Him. Our presence and witness should bring the life of God wherever we go.

The gift of eternal life is freely available to all who come to God by worshiping Jesus as Lord and God and live obeying His Word. There is an inheritance for the people of God prepared by God Himself for those who obey and wait for Him in faithfulness.

Conclusion

Life on earth will draw to its appointed end just as it is written in God's Word and in His time.

Those who choose God have chosen a relationship and a pathway in life that leads to success and fulfilment and an eternity with the God who is love. If we develop a spiritual foundation that includes the teaching and belief in the letter to the Hebrews chapter 6 verses 1-2:

1. Therefore, leaving the discussion of the elementary principles of Christ, let us go on to perfection, not laying again the foundation of repentance from dead works and of faith toward God,
2. of the doctrine of baptisms, of laying on of hands, of resurrection of the dead, and of eternal judgment.

this will help establish a spiritual foundation for life that is not easily shaken. What we believe is the most important thing about us and determines our eternity. Physical death is not the end, it's the entrance to eternity.

References

Vine's Expository Dictionary of Old and New Testament Words, W.E. Vine, Old Testament Edited by F.F. Bruce, World Bible Publishers, Iowa Falls Iowa, 1981

The New Strong's Exhaustive Concordance of the Bible, James Strong, Thomas Nelson Publishers, Nashville, 1984

Other Books by the Author

God's Promise of Healing

Redemption God's Buy Back Plan

www.ingramcontent.com/pod-product-compliance
Lightning Source LLC
Chambersburg PA
CBHW070610010526
44118CB00012B/1482